OSPREY AIRCRAFT OF THE ACES • 22

# Imperial Japanese Navy Aces 1937-45

SERIES EDITOR: TONY HOLMES

OSPREY AIRCRAFT OF THE ACES · 22

# Imperial Japanese Navy Aces 1937-45

Henry Sakaida

OSPREY
AEROSPACE

**Front Cover**
CPO Hiroyoshi Nishizawa of the 251st AG manoeuvres his A6M3 Model 22 into position to deliver a final killing blow to an already smoking Marine Corps F4U Corsair over the Solomons. The great ace recorded his first claim against a Corsair on 7 June 1943 over the Russell Islands, his victim almost certainly being one of three VMF-112 pilots shot down on this date. All of the American pilots were recovered, and the USMC unit itself lodged claims for eight victories. From June through to 21 August 1943, CPO Nishizawa engaged in numerous fierce actions with F4Us over Rendova, Buin and Vella Lavella. During this period, the ace participated in the destruction of 45 Corsairs, which were attributed to his unit rather than him, as per the Japanese Naval Air Force (JNAF) GHQ directive prohibiting individual victory credits
(*Cover painting by Iain Wyllie*)

First published in Great Britain in 1998 by Osprey Publishing
Michelin House, 81 Fulham Road, London SW3 6RB

ISBN 1 85532 727 9

Edited by Tony Holmes
Page design by TT Designs, T & S Truscott
Cover Artwork by Iain Wyllie
Aircraft Profiles by Tom Tullis
Figure Artwork by Mike Chappell
Scale Drawings by Mark Styling

Printed in Hong Kong

ACKNOWLEDGEMENTS
The author wishes to thank Japanese aviation historians Kazuhiko Osuo, Dr Yasuho Izawa and Yasuo Kumoi for their contributions and provision of rare photographs. Thanks are also due to Jiro Yoshida of the Zero Pilots' Association, Yoshio Shiga, Gary Nila, Saburo Sakai and Maru Magazine (Kojinsha Co). Finally, the editor acknowledges the use of photographs from the Aerospace Publishing, Philip Jarrett and Robert C Mikesh collections.

EDITOR'S NOTE
To make this best-selling series as authoritative as possible, the editor would be extremely interested in hearing from any individual who may have relevant photographs, documentation or first-hand experiences relating to the elite pilots, and their aircraft, of the various theatres of war. Any material used will be fully credited to its original source. Please write to Tony Holmes at 10 Prospect Road, Sevenoaks, Kent, TN13 3UA, Great Britain.

# CONTENTS

# THE CHINA WAR

It was inevitable that Japan and China would eventually go to war. Japanese economic ambitions in China and throughout Greater South-East Asia could not be supported without a modern military, and the backbone to any large-scale land occupation lay in the invading force's ability to support such actions through the use of air power. Japan had gained concessions in China by siding with the Western powers in World War 1, and with China itself being politically weak and having little say in governing her own internal affairs, the time was ripe to strike.

The first step to occupation was taken when Japan's Kwantung Army marched into Manchuria and turned it into a puppet state, thus souring relations between the two countries. China appealed to the League of Nations, who started a boycott of Japanese goods. On 18 January 1932 rioting broke out in Shanghai against the invading army, and to quell this disturbance, Japan landed an expeditionary force near the port city.

The first meaningful aerial engagement between the two force occurred on 5 February when two bombers and three fighter escorts from the carrier *Hosho* encountered a Blackburn F.2D Lincock III biplane fighter (one of only two supplied to China) over Shingu. The pilot, Tsu Dah-Shien, played 'tag' with the formation through the clouds until he was hit and wounded after his guns jammed – he managed to return to base.

Also embroiled in this escalating conflict were a handful of mercenary pilots employed by the Chinese to oppose the occupiers, and they were involved in the first real 'bloodletting' on 22 February over the Souchow Railway Station. American mercenary Robert Short, flying a Boeing P-12 biplane, intercepted carrier bombers from the *Kaga* and destroyed the lead aircraft. However, he in turn was duly shot down by a trio of escort

A5M4 Type 96 'Claudes' of the 12th AG are seen flying a patrol over China in 1939. Initially, JNAF pilots were reluctant to transition from the well-liked 'Claude' to the new Zero fighter, as in mock dogfights with the the latter type the Type 96 won every time. However, the spectacular first combat success enjoyed by the Zero in September 1940 eventually changed pilots' minds once and for all (*via Robert C Mikesh*)

pilots, thus becoming the first victory of the JNAF in China. Skirmishing around Shanghai lasted until May when Japanese forces were withdrawn.

By July 1937 relations between the two nations had deteriorated to a point where armed conflict seemed inevitable, and on 7 July a local skirmish between opposing forces on the Marco Polo Bridge, south-west of Beijing, provided the spark to ignite the China War. This event united all Chinese – despite their differing ideologies – against the Japanese.

The state of military aviation in China was very poor, with regional warlords having purchased foreign aircraft on the basis of corruption rather than performance. As a result there was no standard fighter, nor a cohesive organisation. Chinese pilots were not properly trained either, the Chinese Air Force (CAF) also suffering through corruption and political meddling which saw officer pilots owing their allegiance to their local warlords rather than the nation as a whole.

The first large-scale CAF counterattack following invasion occurred on 14 August when then Capt Claire Chennault (acting as operational CO of the fragmented air force under authority of Chiang Kai Shek) launched 60 fighters against the Japanese fleet. CAF aircraft failed to hit any ships

China War veteran Matsuo Hagiri poses with his favourite A5M4 whilst part of the *Soryu* Fighter Squadron
(*via Aerospace Publishing*)

Squadronmates of Matsuo Hagiri pose in front of Hideo Oishi's A5M4 aboard the *Soryu* during a 1939 deployment. Like Hagiri, Oishi was one of the pilots made famous by the audacious Taipingsze airfield attack on 4 October 1940
(*via Aerospace Publishing*)

With their Nakajima Kotobuki 41 engines clattering away, a clutch of 'Claudes' prepare for launch from *Soryu*'s deck during a fleet training exercise in early 1940
(*via Aerospace Publishing*)

in their dismal bombing attacks, Chinese pilots also mistakenly attacking the British cruiser HMS *Cumberland,* but fortunately their bombs fell wide of the vessel. They also dropped bombs into the Shanghai city centre, accidentally killing more than 1700 civilians and wounding a further 1800. In the first JNAF victory of the renewed conflict, a Nakajima floatplane shot down a Curtiss Hawk III. Subsequent bombing raids against Chinese targets in the far interior of the country proved costly for the JNAF, and it didn't take long for Naval GHQ to realise that unescorted bombers were vulnerable to attack from CAF fighters. Conversely, those bomber groups escorted by fighters were seldom attacked.

In September 1937 the Second Combined Air Flotilla returned to Shanghai with a new weapon – the Mitsubishi A5M Type 96 'Claude' monoplane fighter. For the JNAF the age of the biplane was over. With a speed in excess of 250 mph, the 'Claude' out performed any enemy biplane and held its own against the Soviet I-16. Within two months of the the Type 96's introduction, fighter opposition had drastically reduced.

Despite the advent of the 'Claude', Chinese fighters remained active during 1938, aided by aggressive Soviet 'volunteers' in their I-16s. And although it was widely reported in the Japanese press that 1227 CAF were destroyed in 15 months of fighting, the actual number was much less.

The Japanese never expected to conquer all of China, for it was simply too vast. However, they concentrated on holding major cities in the interior and ports along the coast, and by 1940 the war was at a stalemate. Two years earlier, the Japanese government had attempted to negotiate an end to the conflict but had been thwarted by a militant faction of the army and certain influential Chinese who wanted to keep the war going.

In September 1940 the JNAF introduced the new Zero fighter into the combat arena, and contrary to popular belief, pilots were initially not impressed with the new mount, preferring to keep their Type 96s. In mock combats between the Zero and the 'Claude', the old monoplane won every dogfight thanks to it being lighter and more manoeuvrable. It would have to take some extraordinary event to change the pilots' minds.

The first combat between the Zero and CAF fighters occurred on 13 September 1940 over Chunking when 27 I-15s and I-16s were engaged. In the subsequent action the Japanese claimed all 27 fighters destroyed without loss, WO Koshiro Yamashita becoming the first JNAF 'ace in a day' with five kills. The news spread like wildfire, and showed that what the Zero lacked in manoeuvrability when compare with the Claude, it made up for in firepower and speed. Lt Cdr Iyozoh Fujita summed it up best when he said, 'The Type 96 was very easy to control, and in a mock dogfight with a Zero it was superior. But the Zero was better than the Type 96 in total performance, so I liked the Zero'.

The combat experience gained by the JNAF during the China War would later prove to be invaluable to naval aviators during the opening months of the Pacific War, pilots believing that their beloved Zero could out perform any fighter in the world. Navy pilots also boasted that their training was superior to their army counterparts, and proved it time and again by defeating those who rose to the challenge in mock dogfights.

Fired up with naval pride, experienced in combat and with extreme confidence in their new Zero fighter, the JNAF pilot was a dangerous opponent heading into 1941.

## Lieutenant Mochifumi Nango

The elder brother of Japanese Army Air Force (JAAF) pilot Shigeo Nango, Mochifumi emulated his sibling by becoming a model fighter-leader in the JNAF. Born in Hiroshima Prefecture in July 1906 as the son of a rear admiral, it was only natural that Mochifumi would enter the Naval Academy at Etajima – he duly graduated in the 55th Class in 1927, and went on to complete his flight training in November 1932.

Later in the decade Lt Nango went to England and served as an assistant naval attaché at the Japanese Embassy in London. Here, he refined his scholarly manner, improved his English speaking ability and showed a great attention to detail, all of which marked him out as a natural leader.

With the China War only three months old, Lt Nango went into battle as division officer in the 13th Air Group (AG) in October 1937, and it wasn't long before the 31-year-old aviator made a name for himself. On 2 December he led six 'Claudes' against an estimated 30 CAF fighters, downing two himself (out of thirteen claimed) and bringing honours to his unit. CO of the China Area Fleet, Adm Kiyoshi Hasegawa, issued the following citation, dated 5 December 1937, as a result of the engagement;

'The time when the Chinese Air Force was trying to regain its power through aggressive attacks with the latest imported fighters, you (Nango) on 2 December 1937, supported the raid on Nanking and battled 30 enemy fighters which began attacking you and your six fighters. Your unit downed 13 enemy fighters and made them loose spirit. Your continuous contribution to these missions are great. Your military service record is outstanding. You are hereby commended.'

Lt Nango was transferred to the carrier *Soryu* to become division officer later that month, and he served in this capacity until July 1938 when he was moved to the newly-organised 15th AG to become group leader. Based on land at Anking, his group flew both ground support missions for army troops against Hankow and air defence patrols to protect shipping along the Yangtze River. A rudimentary forward airfield with few creature comforts, the unsanitary conditions at Anking brought illness to the pilots of the new unit, Nango included. However, he refused to be side-lined and continued to fly missions. It was to have its consequences.

On 18 July 1938, whilst flying over Lake Poyang, Lt Nango dived on an I-15 piloted by Soviet volunteer Valentin Dudonov. The Russian was unaware that he was under attack until bullets started striking his seat armour plate. Before he could react, the JNAF pilot crashed into his fighter, and although Dudonov baled out and survived, Nango was killed when his shattered 'Claude' plunged into the lake. The cause of Nango's collision was attributed to vision problems brought on by ill health – he had been unable to judge the separation distance.

Eight victories have been attributed to *Gunshin Nango Shosa* (War God Lt Cdr Nango).

## Warrant Officer Kiyoto Koga

The honour of becoming the first JNAF ace belongs to Kiyoto Koga, who was born in Fukuoka Prefecture in June 1910. Exactly 17 years later he joined the navy at Sasebo, and in May 1931 became a fighter pilot.

Lt Mochifumi Nango was one of the JNAF's most accomplished fighter-leaders during the China War. A scholar and a gentleman, who spoke excellent English, his devotion to duty eventually cost him his life in July 1938 (*K Osuo*)

Kiyoto Koga became the first ace of the JNAF on 24 November 1937 when he shot down an I-16 over Nanking. As a result of this achieve-ment he received a rare personal citation from the CO of the China Area Fleet, Adm Kiyoshi Hasegawa. Seen as an excellent role model for young aviation trainees, Koga was sent home to work as an instructor in early 1938, but was subsequently killed in a flying accident in September of that same year (*K Osuo*)

PO2/c Saburo Sakai smiles for the camera in his Type 96 'Claude' at Hankow airfield, in China, in September 1939. As can be gauged from this view, the open cockpit of the Mitsubishi fighter afforded the pilot excellent all-round visibility. A month after this photo was taken, Sakai became a national hero when, on 3 October 1939, he single-hand-edly pursued 12 DB-3 bombers for over 150 miles before finally shoot-ing one down (*S Sakai*)

As a member of the 13th AG, Koga was stationed in Shanghai for about a month after the outbreak of the China War, and he enjoyed his first aer-ial successes during his first encounter with the CAF on 19 September 1937 – two Curtiss Hawks fell to his guns over Nanking. Three days later, Koga downed a further pair of Hawks. On 24 November, he became an ace according to Western standards when he downed an I-16 over Nanking, and he continued his scoring run into December with a bomber (on the 2nd) and three I-16s(on the 9th) over Nanchang.

For distinguished service in the air war over China, Adm Kiyoshi Hasegawa awarded Koga with a personal citation on 31 December 1937, noting his destruction of 11 fighters and two bombers. At the same time, the honouree was promoted to warrant officer.

A veteran of many aerial engagements, WO Kiyoto Koga died on 16 September 1938 from injuries received during a crash 24 hours earlier whilst conducting night training exercises with the Yokosuka AG.

His score of 13 victories was officially recognised.

## Warrant Officer Kanichi Kashimura

During the height of every armed conflict, a need arises to promote an outstanding individual as a role model for the rank and file. Kanichi Kashimura served this purpose in China, becoming known as 'the pilot who returned on one wing'.

Born in Kagawa Prefecture, Japan, in July 1913, he joined the Navy and graduated from flight training in July 1934. In October 1937, Kashimura was transferred to the 13th AG, where he saw combat for the first time on 22 November and downed two aircraft over Nanking.

On 9 December PO3/c Kashimura fought Curtiss Hawks over Nan-chang, destroying one and then colliding with another aircraft (an unknown type that could have been either Japanese or Chinese), tearing off a third of his left wing. Through superb piloting, the calm aviator brought his crippled 'Claude' back to base, and after four landing attempts, the aircraft somersaulted on touching the ground on its fourth approach and lost its tail in the subsequent crash. Astoundingly, the pilot walked away from the wreckage unharmed. Local news reporters quickly sent the story back to Japan, where Kashimura gained instant fame.

PO3/c Kanichi Kashimura collided with an unidentified aircraft during aerial combat on 9 December 1937 and returned with a third of his left wing missing. News reports of his heroic struggle to make it back to base quickly spread throughout Japan, and his example of tenacity and fighting spirit was later used to inspire a new generation of naval fighter pilots (*K Osuo*)

Kashimura's Type 96 (No 4-115) was photographed from the ground as he made several landing attempts at an airfield in Shanghai. Although the aircraft violently somersaulted onto its back upon making contact with the ground, the pilot walked away without as much as a scratch (*K Osuo*)

Having completed his tour with the *Soryu* Fighter Squadron (see photo on page seven), Matsuo 'Mustachio' Hagiri joined the Zero-equipped 12th AG and went on to became a popular and daring fighter pilot over China – where he gained most of his victories. However, his greatest contribution to the JNAF would come during the final years of World War 2 when he was pressed into the role of test pilot (*M Hagiri*)

After achieving eight victories over China, Kashimura was reassigned to the Yokosuka AG in March 1938. Once back in Japan, 'Kashimura, The Pilot Who Returned On One Wing' served as a living role model for future generation of naval aviators. Back in China for his second tour of duty by the end of 1939, he found that activity by the CAF had all but ceased, and he returned to instructional duties at Yokosuka without having scored further kills.

Kashimura was promoted to warrant officer in October 1942, and in December of that year was posted to the 582nd AG and left for service in New Guinea. Once in-theatre he was quickly back in combat, this time testing his skills against a far more formidable enemy. On 6 March 1943 WO Kashimura failed to return from a mission that had seem him escorting 'Val' dive-bombers on a raid on the Russell Islands. P-39s from the USAAF's 67th Fighter Squadron (FS) concentrated their attacks on the 'Vals' and therefore claimed no Zeroes. However, two A6Ms did fail to return, although only a single claim against a Zero was recorded on this date – Marine SBD gunner S/Sgt Robert H Banner of VMSB-132 claimed to have shot down an A6M 15 miles south-east of the Russells. Kashimura may have been his victim.

WO Kanichi Kashimura achieved 12 recognised aerial victories.

## Lieutenant(jg) Matsuo Hagiri

Matsuo Hagiri contributed to the JNAF's war effort both as a fighter and test pilot. Born in Shizuoka Prefecture in November 1913, he worked as a fireman before joining the navy, graduating from flight training in August 1935.

Exactly five years later Hagiri – as a member of the 12th AG – participated in the first combat mission in which the new Zero fighter was flown. This historic sortie took place on 19 August when Lt Tomotsu Yokoyama led a dozen A6Ms on a bomber escort mission to Chunking. Although no aerial combat took place, the mission did establish a new distance record for a single-engined fighter of over 1000 nautical miles.

As detailed earlier, the Zero's famous dogfighting debut on 13 September 1940 gave such a tremendous boost to the confidence of its pilots that some (like Hagiri) became very cocky with their new mounts. A perfect example of this occurred on 4 October when Hagiri participated in a highly publicised stunt that saw him and three comrades land on the enemy airfield of Taipingsze, at Chengtu, and attempt to vandalise parked aircraft and set the base command post alight! Escaping in a hail of small arms fire, but still not content with his part in the escapade, Hagiri then single-handedly attacked three fighters and downed two of them.

Following the introduction of the Zero, CAF pilots wisely chose to avoid combat with it at all costs, leaving Hagiri with little opportunity to increase his score, which stood at seven by the time he returned to Japan.

In July 1943 WO Hagiri was assigned to the 204th AG and sent to the Solomons, where his main opposition comprised F4U Corsairs and P-38s. Because of his experience, he often flew as flight leader.

On 23 September 1943 the 204th sortied 27 Zeroes to thwart an Allied raid on their anti-aircraft positions south-west of Kahili Airfield. Two squadrons of Marine Corsairs (VMF-213 and -214) attacked the airfield while Australian P-40s escorted the slower-moving SBDs and TBFs. WO Hagiri claimed two F4Us, but was in turn so severely wounded that he had to be sent back to Japan for further treatment.

As the war situation deteriorated for the Japanese, Hagiri was pressed into service as a test pilot, and when B-29s started to raid the Tokyo region he once again flew combat missions. In April 1945 he was wounded by Superfortress gunners and never flew again.

In a distinguished career, Lt(jg) Matsuo Hagiri shot down 13 enemy aircraft. He passed away on 15 January 1997.

## Lieutenant(jg) Tetsuzo Iwamoto

The top ace of the JNAF in both the China and Pacific Wars was Tetsuzo Iwamoto, whose amazing seven-year career was revealed postwar both through his combat diary and by eyewitnesses.

A cunning pilot who favoured 'hit and run' tactics, Iwamoto was born in June 1916 as the third son in a family of three boys and a girl fathered by a Hokkaido Prefecture policeman. As a student of the Masuda Agricultural and Forestry High School, young Tetsu developed into a very opinionated individual, whose stubborn and righteous views caused consternation with his teachers and, eventually, with his military superiors.

With no aspirations of becoming a farmer, Iwamoto secretly enlisted in the navy in June 1934 after telling his parents that he was off to take the college entrance examinations – his parents were left extremely disappointed as they were counting on him to help on the family farm.

Iwamoto elected to become a fighter pilot rather than remaining a common seaman for aviators enjoyed special privileges. He took the difficult entrance examination and passed, being accepted into flight training and graduating in December 1936.

The future 'ace-of-aces' showed his ability right from the start. As a member of the 12th AG, his baptism of fire came on 25 February 1938 over Nanchang, China, when A1/c Iwamoto's flight was jumped by enemy I-15 and I-16 fighters whilst on a bomber escort mission. In the wild melee that followed, the young 22-year-old claimed four fighters shot down and one probable. Iwamoto repeated this performance on 29 April

Tetsuzo Iwamoto (shown here in 1945 as an ensign) became not only the top JNAF ace of the China War, but also World War 2. Immune to life-threatening (in a fighter pilot at least) traits like blind spirit and bravado, he favoured 'hit and run' tactics, and knew when to fight and when to run (*Y Izawa*)

over Hankow, when he again downed four fighters and was duly rewarded a citation from his CO for being the top pilot of the day.

In September 1938 Iwamoto was ordered back to Japan, where he became a member of the Saiki AG. With 14 kills in China, 'Tetsu' was the top JNAF ace of the conflict.

PO1/c Iwamoto was subsequently posted to the carrier *Zuikaku*, and on the opening day of the Pacific War he flew protective cover over the strike force as they launched their aircraft against Pearl Harbor. Iwamoto returned to Japan on 24 December, and later participated in battles over the Indian Ocean and Coral Sea. In August 1942 he was pressed into service as an instructor, as the disaster at Midway necessitated the mass training of replacement pilots.

Whilst Iwamoto feverishly trained new naval aviators, the Japanese bastion at Rabaul, New Britain, had been bearing the brunt of a massive US bombing campaign. Aircraft from the US Fifth and Thirteenth Air Forces had worn down the number of Zero fighters, and accompanying pilots, to a dangerous level, and as part of the reinforcement CPO Iwamoto was ordered to lead a formation of 15 replacement Zeroes to Rabaul in November. Once in-theatre, he became a member of the 253rd AG, and he and his men engaged the Americans on a daily basis.

On 17 November Iwamoto encountered the F4U Corsair for the first time during a strike on Torokina, his opponents being part of VF-17 'Jolly Rogers' (see *Aircraft of the Aces 8 - Corsair Aces of World War 2* for further details). Although the Japanese attack on Torokina was unsuccessful, Iwamoto claimed two of the navy Corsairs.

The New Year brought more American attacks, and following the huge carrier air strike against Truk Island on 16-17 February, the JNAF was forced to withdraw all serviceable aircraft from Rabaul. As part of the exodus, Iwamoto flew to Truk with the remnants of the 253rd, the unit

Also a veteran of the *Soryu* Fighter Squadron, PO1/c Hideo Oishi adds two victory markings to the impressive tail scoreboard of his 12th AG Zero No 3-173 at Hankow airfield – he had downed two enemy aircraft with this combat-seasoned A6M2 on 14 March 1941 over Chengtu. PO3/c Hatsumasa Yamatani had started the aircraft's scoring run by claiming four victories on 13 September 1940 during the type's 'baptism of fire'. Others who contributed to the tally included PO2/c Miyakuni Kamidaira and PO3/c Seiji Hiramoto (*K Osuo*)

Another veteran A6M2 Zero of the 12th AG, this aircraft wears 28 kill markings on its tail. Having survived many months in combat, the aircraft was finally taken out of frontline service in June 1941 and donated to the Naval Academy at Etajima for display purposes (*K Osuo*)

This 14th AG A6M2 Zero Model 11 (serial No 9-182) was photographed over southern China in the autumn of 1940. The aircraft later participated in a vicious combat with enemy I-15/-16s and Curtiss Hawks over Kunming on 14 July 1941, after which the Zero pilots claimed to have destroyed 13 aircraft in just 15 minutes without loss (*via Phil Jarrett*)

immediately being thrust into action against B-24s which bombed the island on a near-daily basis.

Iwamoto returned to Japan in June 1944, but in October he was sent to fight over Formosa and the Philippines. By that stage the war situation had grown so desperate that he flew solo missions strafing beach landings and airfields at night – achieving very little, he was eventually sent home.

In early 1945 Iwamoto was transferred to the 203rd AG and fought against B-29s and carrier fighters attacking Kyushu, as well as seeing action over Okinawa. He spent the remaining months of the war training young flyers for the final *kamikaze* suicide attack at Iwakuni Airfield.

Totally disillusioned at his country's surrender, Iwamoto could not adjust to postwar Japan. He did various jobs but was never content, turning instead to alcohol, which caused many personal problems. The great ace died in 1955 aged just 38 due to septicaemia caused by a series of surgical operations on his back for a war wound.

Iwamoto kept an elaborate diary during his career, and by his own reckoning he had claimed some of the following – seven F4Fs, four P-38s, 48 F4Us, two P-39s, one P-40, 29 F6Fs, one P-47, one P-51, four Spitfires, 48 SBDs (plus another 30 by aerial burst bombs) and eight B-25s. Whilst flying from Rabaul he claimed 142 aerial victories out of a final tally of 202 destroyed, 26 shared, 22 unconfirmed, two damaged and two destroyed on the ground. Postwar Japanese historians have listed Iwamoto with 'just' 80 victories, but the true figure will never be known.

## Lieutenant(jg) Watari Handa

Watari Handa was a famous veteran of the China War whose brilliant skills were not fully realised in World War 2 due to a combination of bad luck and health problems. Born in Fukuoka Prefecture in August 1912, he joined the navy in 1928, and after graduation from flight training in 1933, served both on the carrier *Ryujo* and with various land-based units.

Shortly after the start of the China War in August 1937, Handa saw action flying from the *Kaga* over Shanghai, duly recording his first aerial victory (a Hawk) on 9 September – 11 days later he destroyed three more aircraft over Nanking. In June of the following year Handa was transferred to the 15th AG and returned to action, this time over Nanchang. By the time he had finished his tour of duty in November his tally had risen to 15 (six officially recognised), and upon returning to Japan he was promoted to warrant officer. Handa's next assignment saw him instructing new flight trainees at Tsuchiura Air Base.

When the ace was posted to the Tainan AG in February 1942 he was already 30 years of age, which was considered to be somewhat old for an operational fighter pilot. Nevertheless, he brought his fame and a wealth of combat experience to the unit, and his presence was most welcome.

However, an incident on 13 May 1942 demoralised WO Handa and ended his flying career. He requested the loan of fellow ace Saburo Sakai's wingman, PO3/c Toshiaki Honda, for a recce mission over the enemy airfield at Port Moresby. Despite Honda's protest, Sakai ordered him to go, and when the three Zeroes were subsequently ambushed by P-39s over Seven Mile Strip, he was killed. Broken in spirit and blaming himself for Honda's loss, Handa was never able to regain his old touch, and upon

Lt(jg) Watari Handa became a great ace in China, but a flying incident in 1942 broke his spirit and ruined his career (*Y Izawa*)

being diagnosed with tuberculosis, he returned to Japan in late 1942.

Lt(jg) Watari Handa scored 15+ kills (13 officially) and died in 1948. On his deathbed he told his wife, 'I have fought bravely all my life, but I could never forgive myself for having lost Sakai's wingman at Lae'.

## Warrant Officer Toshio Kuroiwa

Toshio Kuroiwa made his mark in JNAF history by claiming a share in the navy's first aerial kill. Born in Fukuoka Prefecture in 1908, he enlisted in 1926 and graduated from flight training two years later.

Tension between Japan and China led to the first Shanghai Incident of 1932, which saw the boycotting of Japanese goods result in riots in Shanghai. Shots were exchanged and the Japanese overreacted by sending an armed expeditionary force to protect their interests – Toshio Kuroiwa was part of that force aboard the carrier *Kaga*.

The first air-to-air combat between Chinese and Japanese fighters occurred on 22 February 1932 over the Souchow Railroad Station when three B1M3 carrier bombers and three A1N2 Type 3 biplane fighters were attacked by a lone Boeing P-12, flown by American mercenary Robert Short. Unaware of the escorts, Short attacked and shot down a bomber, but almost immediately Lt Nokiji Ikuta, Leading Seaman Kazuo Takeo and PO3/c Toshio Kuroiwa pounced on the brash American, sending him to a fiery death. The three men were officially credited with the Japanese military's first aerial kill and received citations.

During the China War, Kuroiwa was attached to the 12th AG and saw considerable action in 1938. With his wild antics in the air, he cultivated a 'bad boy' image, which his superiors tolerated because of his skill. Having turned 31 by the time his tour of duty ended in 1939, Kuroiwa was considered to be to old for further frontline flying, so he left active duty and gained employment flying airliners instead.

Toshio Kuroiwa disappeared off the Malay Peninsula on 26 August 1944 during a transport flight. His score of 13 was officially recognised.

PO Kuroiwa was one of the oldest fighter pilots of the China War, having first seen action in 1932 as one of a trio of men credited with Japan's premier aerial victory (*Y Izawa*)

A6M2 Model 11s of the 12th AG fly over the cloud-shrouded Chinese mainland on 26 May 1941. The aircraft marked with the double stripe was the personal mount of China veteran Lt Minoru Suzuki, whilst the second fighter was being flown by PO3/c Kunimori Nakakariya, who survived the war with 16 kills (*via Aerospace Publishing*)

# EARLY MONTHS OF THE PACIFIC WAR

**W**hen Japan unleashed the might of its military forces against the Americans at Pearl Harbor and in the Philippines, it did so with the most modern aircraft and highly-trained pilots that it possessed at any time in its history. While some units in the JNAF were still flying Type 96 'Claudes', all of the fighter aircraft committed to the Pearl Harbor and Philippines missions were A6M2 Zeroes, many of which were flown by veterans of the China War.

The conflict in the Pacific grew out of economic and political discontent felt in Japan against 'Western Imperialists' – namely the United States and Britain. Japan's successful forays into Manchuria and China had allowed its military to test and perfect its arsenal of offensive weapons, especially its fighters and bombers. It also allowed JNAF and JAAF aircrew to perfect tactics that would give them the advantage over the air arms of the Western powers in the first critical months of war.

Success on the Chinese mainland throughout the 1930s led Japan's military leaders to grow overconfident in their forces' ability to wage war on a much larger scale in Asia, this overconfidence manifesting itself in the dramatic upsurge of fanatical nationalism that swept the nation.

By the summer of 1941 Japanese leaders knew that conflict was inevitable, and so ordered their forces to prepare for war whilst the politicians still it carried out diplomatic negotiations in Washington DC. Adm

Lt Saburo Shindo, flying AI-102, starts his take-off run alomg the deck of the *Akagi* as part of the second wave attack on Pearl Harbor. Shindo served as division officer within the carrier squadron at this time, and was one of the few Pearl Harbor veterans to survive the war (*via Aerospace Publishing*)

Isoroku Yamamoto, C-in-C of the Combined Forces, was given orders to undertake an all-out assault on US forces at Pearl Harbor, in the Hawaiian Islands. The date of the strike was set for 8 December 1941, and his force was comprised of 23 warships, including six fleet aircraft carriers, and 350+ aircraft.

By the time political negotiations failed, the carriers had already positioned themselves some 200 nautical miles north of Pearl Harbor. At 0130 (Tokyo time) bombers began roaring off the flightdecks.

Zero pilots played a key role in assuring the success of the surprise assault. In order to prevent the vulnerable torpedo- and dive-bombers being molested as they manoeuvred into position to make their runs, A6Ms strafed parked aircraft and shot down any that managed to launch. Not all of the Americans who sortied were 'easy pickings', however.

Lt Iyozoh Fujita found himself under attack as he led his men toward Wheeler Field, and in the wild dogfight that ensued, Japanese aviators were taken aback by the aggressiveness of their American counterparts – their opponents could have been 2Lts George Welch and Ken Taylor of the 47th Pursuit Squadron (PS), flying P-40Bs. Fujita poured fire into an aircraft below him, which smoked but escaped. Not wishing to push his luck any further, Fujita signalled to his men to withdraw and head

PO3/c Shimpei Sano clears *Akagi*'s island in A6M2 Zero 21 AI-111 as he too launches with the second wave attackers bound for Pearl Harbor. Sano was later killed during the Battle of Midway (*Maru*)

A6M2s of *Shokaku*'s fighter squadron run up as the carrier sails into wind for a dawn launch north-east of Hawaii. Six Zeroes from this unit participated in the first wave attack, strafing Kaneohe and Bellows airfields (*via Aerospace Publishing*)

Sporting ten cherry blossoms, the tail of Zero X-183 reveals the score of PO2/c Yoshiro Hashiguchi, who saw action with the 3rd AG over the Dutch East Indies at the start of the Pacific War. He later enjoyed further success over Darwin, Rabaul, and Guadalcanal. Attaining the rank of chief petty officer, Hashiguchi was finally posted missing in action on 25 October 1944 when his carrier was sunk. He achieved over ten victories (*K Osuo*)

Two great aces are seen as student pilots in this May 1941 class photo. Takeo Tanimizu (standing, second from right) and Shoichi Sugita (standing to Tanimizu's left) were classmates at Tsukuba Air Base, where they flew the Type 93 Intermediate Trainer, seen here as a backdrop. Their class graduated in March 1942 – prior to the Midway disaster. Subsequent training was notably inferior as the JNAF rushed to graduate pilots to make good the Midway losses (*T Tanimizu*)

towards the rendezvous area.

The attacking force suffered casualties amounting to 55 officers and enlisted men during the Pearl Harbor raid, with remarkably few of this number being fighter pilots – just nine Zeroes were lost to all causes (three in the first strike and six in the second). There was no wild jubilation or celebration at their success, however, the weary aviators simply being relieved that they had survived their first day of war. They also grieved for their comrades who had not returned.

The Pearl Harbor attack had been a spectacular success, for the US fleet in the western Pacific had been crippled with one bold stroke and the enlisted men and officers of the JNAF now considered themselves invincible. However, senior men at Naval GHQ (including Adm Yamamoto himself) were far from elated, for they had failed to catch their primary targets at anchor – aircraft carriers. They would come back to hurt them.

Japanese Navy Academy graduates were open-minded and worldly wise, differing greatly from their army counterparts. In their cruises to the West as midshipmen, they saw firsthand the industrial might and capabilities of the great economic superpowers, leading some to secretly believe that Japan could never win this new war.

Coinciding with the strike at Pearl Harbor, Japanese forces launched an all-out attack in the Philippines, Hong Kong and the Dutch East Indies – with very little in the way of natural resources, Japan need the oil reserves, rubber and mineral wealth of the Dutch East Indies to fuel its war effort.

From their base in Formosa, the Tainan and 3rd AGs raided Clark and Iba airfields in the Philippines in advance of the bombers, thus neutralising any fighter opposition. Despite the warnings radioed to their forces in the Philippines during the Pearl Harbor attack, the Americans were once again caught unprepared, resulting in the USAAC losing half of it aircraft destroyed or damaged in one raid.

Veteran fighter pilots like POs Kuniyoshi Tanaka, Saburo Sakai, Kaneyoshi Muto and WO Sadaaki Akamatsu tangled with P-40s in lopsided dogfights, although the majority of American aircraft were destroyed on the ground. With another raid on 10 December, US air power in the Philippines was decisively crushed.

The success of these lightning strikes further boosted the morale of the JNAF, the missions setting a new distance record for the Zero. The entire round-trip distance from Formosa to the Philippines covered more than 1000 miles, and it was such an incredible distance for a single-engined aircraft that the Americans believed that they had flown from carriers – strict flight formation and fuel conservation training had paid off handsomely.

With the Philippines neutralised, the JNAF directed their attention to the Dutch East Indies. Attempting to defend the latter was the RAF, the Netherlands East Indies Army Air Force and surviving elements of the USAAC, and although they fought to near annihilation to thwart the invasion, they were overwhelmed by a superior enemy. Dutch F2A Buffaloes and Hawks, in particular, proved to be little more than 'cannon fodder' for the A6M2s, as Saburo Sakai later noted, 'The Buffaloes were rough, inferior, aircraft. They never stood a chance against our Zeroes.'

RAF Hurricanes and P-40s of the USAAC's 20th PS faired a little better than the Buffaloes, but the destruction of their airfields (and critical supplies and aircraft) allied with the total confusion and panic on the ground prevented them from effectively mounting an organised counter-attack. The Java campaign concluded in the first week of March 1942 when organised resistance ceased, and thousands of Allied soldiers surrendered. Once again air support had proven to be pivotal in the Japanese *blitzkrieg* of the early months of the Pacific War. Now the JNAF turned their attention to New Guinea and Australia.

PO2/c Yoshiro Hashiguchi is seen seated in his A6M2 Zero X-183 whilst part of the 3rd AG in late 1941. The aircraft's rudimentary ring-bead gunsight is just visible in this photograph
(*via Aerospace Publishing*)

The last sight that many an Allied pilot glimpsed in his rear-vision mirror prior to being shot down during the early months of the Pacific War. This particular Zero is a clipped-wing A6M3 Model 32, examples of which reached the frontline just in time for the Japanese foray across the Asia-Pacific rim
(*via Aerospace Publishing*)

work by striking the vessel twice with torpedoes, the stubborn carrier refused to die – on 6 June a third torpedo from a Japanese submarine finally sent *Yorktown* to the bottom.

The battle was not quite over, however, for aircraft from the *Enterprise* located the surviving Japanese carrier *Hiryu* and quickly reduced her to a gutted hulk. She was scuttled by her crew the following morning.

The loss of four fleet carriers, experienced pilots and aircrew and entire squadrons in a single engagement stunned the Japanese. In the subsequent scramble to make good their aviation losses, the JNAF recalled many veteran pilots from land-based units across the occupied territories back to Japan to serve as instructors. The mass training of pilots quickly began in earnest, but in order return units to their previous strengths, the entrance requirements were lowered and the flight training syllabus shortened – these factors combined to produce pilots ill-equipped for frontline flying. The JNAF would pay dearly for Midway.

## Lieutenant Commander Iyozoh Fujita

Iyozoh Fujita was one of two naval aviators who was recognised as having shot down ten enemy aircraft in one day. The son of a doctor and a midwife, he was born in Shantung Province, China, in November 1917. He became interested in pursuing a naval career while attending high school, where his scholastic aptitude earned him entrance into the Naval Academy at Etajima in the Class of 1938. The young ensign completed flight training in June 1940.

When the Japanese attacked Pearl Harbor on 7 December 1941, Lt(jg) Fujita sortied from the carrier *Soryu* as a flight leader in the second wave fighter escort. He strafed ground targets and his Zero was hit by return fire, and as related in the previous chapter, while gathering the escorts for their return, his formation was jumped by either P-36s or P-40s and a wild dogfight ensued. Managing to disengage from the action in his damaged Zero, Fujita led his men back to the carrier where, upon landing, a piece of his engine broke off.

JNAF pilots entered 1942 in high spirits and with total confidence in the Zero. At the time a naval aviator needed to have completed between 50-100 hours' flying time and four-five landings to achieve carrier qualification, and even the youngest fleet pilot had at least 500 flight hours.

One of those pilots entering the Midway action buoyed by his previous success was Lt Iyozoh Fujita. He carried this confidence into action with him on 4 June when he intercepted a large number of torpedo-bombers during a combat air patrol over the carrier task force. Directed into position by shipboard radio vectoring, Fujita chose the previously untried tactic of diving headlong into the formation rather than attacking the group from the rear. Sweeping through with his guns continuously blazing, he was stunned to see two or three aircraft falling away smoking.

'This is the method!' Fujita exclaimed as he continued his attacks, subsequently shooting down four torpedo-bombers (three jointly) and three fighters (two jointly). Unfortunately, his aircraft was then hit by friendly fire and he had to ditch in the sea. Bobbing up and down in high waves with no hope of rescue, he resigned himself to death, but fortunately his was picked up after just four hours in the water by a destroyer.

Lt Iyozoh Fujita found his shooting eye during the Battle of Midway, becoming a double ace in just one day. He is one of just a handful of Pearl Harbor Zero pilots to have survived the war (*Maru*)

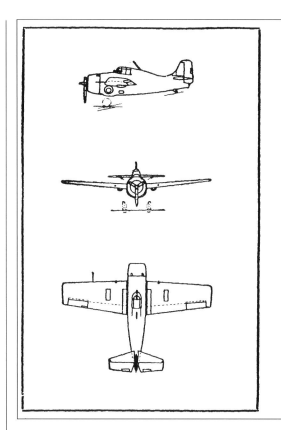

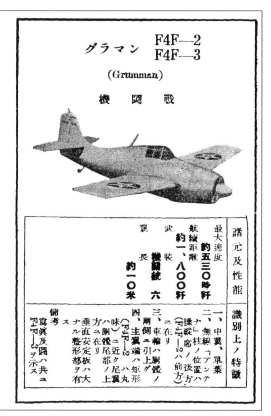

'After Midway, many surviving pilots were pulled out to become instructors', lamented Fujita. 'Removing veteran pilots from frontline units caused us to loose fighting strength. In the end, it was a tremendous burden for our pilots. I think about ten per cent of our veteran pilots were lost at Midway.'

The next assignment for Lt Fujita was as division officer on the carrier *Hiyo*. He saw combat in the Solomons and at Guadalcanal, and in November 1943 was appointed group leader of the 301st AG, under the command of Cdr Katsutoshi Yagi.

As an experienced frontline pilot, Lt Fujita made repeated requests for better armament and gunsights, and although manufacturers listened to his recommendations, few if any improvements came forth.

Prior to the end of the war, Lt Fujita fought in the battles at Iwo Jima, Formosa and in defence of the home islands. He ended the war at Fukuchiyama airfield, waiting for the final all-out attack against the invading Americans which never materialised.

Lt Cdr Fujita's final kill total is unclear, as according to historians he achieved 11 victories, whilst other sources place his score at 42. 'I shot at that many, and my bullets did hit them, but how many went down, I don't know', says this modest gentleman. The number of recognised destroyed was seven.

Postwar, Iyozoh Fujita flew as a pilot for Japan Air Lines before retiring in 1978. The past president of the Zero Fighter Pilots Association, he was a guest panelist at the Battle of Midway Symposium held at NAS Pensacola in 1988. He currently resides in Tokyo.

These documents formed part of the official JNAF wartime recognition publication used by all units to instruct pilots on the shape and performance of their foes

# NEW GUINEA, RABAUL AND THE SOLOMONS

I n January 1942, Japanese forces invaded the South-east Pacific islands of New Britain and New Ireland after carrier pilots from VAdm Chuichi Nagumo's task force had quickly overwhelmed the defenders at Rabaul, on New Britain, and Kavieng, on New Ireland. They also destroyed the enemy's air defenses at Lae and Salamaua, along the north-eastern coast of New Guinea.

In order to isolate Australia from the USA, it was also necessary to conquer the Australian garrison at Port Moresby, so the JNAF poured aircraft into Rabaul, whilst advance contingents of fighters and bombers were positioned even closer to the target at forward bases at Lae and Salamaua.

Spearheading the aerial assault against Port Moresby (commencing on 24 February 1942) was the 4th AG, which was joined in March by the Tainan AG at Rabaul – the latter group moved the following month to Lae, and from then on aerial action was brisk as many young neophytes who had participated in the one-sided actions over the Philippines and the Dutch East Indies became hardened veterans fighting the Australians and the Americans. And while pilots from both sides claimed an extraordinary number of kills, loss records painted a more conservative picture.

Bravery and skill were exhibited by pilots on both sides, and victories were hard won. Saburo Sakai, who was the senior enlisted pilot in the Sasai Squadron of the Tainan AG, later spoke of their difficulties in-theatre; 'Our 20 mm cannons were big, heavy and slow firing. It was extremely hard to hit a moving target. Shooting down an enemy aircraft

This panoramic view illustrates just how rudimentary the facilities were at Rabaul for the Tainan AG in 1942. An important staging area for JNAF aircraft in the Solomons, the airfield at Rabaul was used as a central base for satellite strips at Lae (New Guinea) and Buin (Bougainville) (*Sakaida*)

Mechanics labour over a Zero 21 at Lakunai airfield as Mt Hanabuki belches smoke in the background – the active volcano being a familiar landmark for pilots approaching Rabaul. Field modifications performed on the Zero included sawing off the radio mast and removing the useless radio to in order to save weight (*Maru*)

was like hitting a dragonfly with a rifle! It was never easy to score . . .our opponents were tough!'

The Japanese force, set to invade Port Moresby was turned back during the Battle of the Coral Sea on 7 May, its defeat allowing the defenders to quickly reinforce their ranks. Jungle warfare raged on while both sides incessantly attacked each other's airfields and supply depots. The nature of the jungle terrain and myriad tropical diseases also inflicted casualties on both sides.

On 7 August the 1st Marine Division landed on Guadalcanal, this audacious attack stunning the Japanese at Rabaul. To counter the threat, missions previously flown against targets in New Guinea were quickly redirected to Guadalcanal, resulting in Zero pilots at Rabaul flying their longest missions to date – a round-trip of over 1100 miles. The Japanese counterattack proved unsuccessful, however, with the Americans pouring enough men and equipment into the region to overwhelm the defenders on Guadalcanal. In the skies overhead, US Navy and Marine Corps F4Fs exacted a heavy toll on Japanese units, with even modestly damaged aircraft seldom making it back to Rabaul. By February 1943 Guadalcanal had fallen.

As the Allied Forces moved quickly up 'The Slot', so the Japanese retreated to Bougainville. In the wake of the defeat Naval GHQ ceded the defence of New Guinea to the army, JAAF units duly leaving Rabaul so as to provide aerial support for their forces at Wewak and other bases.

On 18 April 1943 the navy suffered a further crippling blow when P-38s from Guadalcanal ambushed a flight of two 'Betty' bombers and six Zero escorts over Bougainville (see Osprey *Aircraft of the Aces 14 - P-38 Lightning Aces of the Pacific and CBI* for further details). In one of the bombers was Adm Yamamoto, C-in-C of the Combined Fleet. News of the admiral's death was greeted with shock in Japan, and it severely rocked the morale of the men in the frontline.

Although the 204th AG continued to oppose Allied intrusions up the Solomons chain, it too was decimated during long-range missions to Guadalcanal. Whilst attempting to defend their bases at their bases at Buin and Kahili from marauding B-24s, JNAF pilots were quickly set upon by overwhelming numbers of escorting P-38s, P-40s and F4Us. To add to their already desperate plight, many veteran Zero pilots were badly weakened by malaria and other tropical ailments, allowing them to be easily shot out of the sky by their relatively novice opponents.

In October 1943 the 201st and 204th AGs were pulled out of Bougainville and sent to Rabaul. During the last few days of that month reinforcement aircraft from New Ireland, Japan and aircraft carriers flooded into the airfields.

The beginning of the end for the JNAF on Rabaul commenced on 12

October when the USAAF's Fifth Air Force sent a force of over 350 aircraft to bomb the great stronghold into submission. Low flying B-25s and Beaufighters strafed the airfields, B-24 'heavies' bombed shipping in Simpson Harbour and P-38s roamed the skies looking for enemy fighters. A series of heavy raids in October and November further reduced Japanese aircraft stocks on Rabaul, and shattered the defenders' morale.

CPO Tetsuzo Iwamoto – the top scoring ace at Rabaul – remarked; 'Prior to the beginning of 1943, we still had hope and fought fiercely. But now, we fought to uphold our honour. We didn't want to become cowards . . . We believed that we were expendable, that we were all going to die. There was no hope of survival – no one cared anymore.'

The harsh tropical environment added to the decline of the JNAF at Rabaul, for unlike their Allied counterparts, the Japanese failed to control the mosquito problem which devastated whole units with malaria. The Allies, on the other hand, sprayed and dusted their bases frequently with the insecticide DDT, which was unavailable to the Japanese. The latter also lacked quinine (the anti-malaria medicine) and its synthetic substitute Atebin. Even if these had been available, Allied submarines and aircraft greatly reduced the number of cargo ships bringing medical supplies to Rabaul. So bad was the malaria problem that many veteran Zero pilots claimed that ill health was the leading cause of casualties at Rabaul.

Carrier pilots, who were not exposed to these health problems at sea, adopted a slightly more positive attitude, which often helped them to survive. PO Takeo Tanimizu explains; 'Fate determines at birth when and where you will die. Since there was nothing I could do about it, I didn't worry too much about dying, and concentrated on my duty.'

Those who survived their first encounters with US fighters over Rabaul quickly recognised the enemy's weaknesses. Tanimizu remembers;

'P-38s at low altitude were easy prey. They were not very fast, so they usually stayed at higher altitudes. Then, they'd swoop down on you, fire, and zoom up. You really had to be careful and keep looking up. Their weakest spot was their tail. A 20 mm hit and their tails would snap off. The only time you could shoot down a Sikorsky (F4U) was when it was fleeing. You had to shoot at it from a certain angle (from the rear, high position, into the cockpit). Otherwise the bullets would bounce off.'

Fellow carrier ace CPO Sadamu Komachi survived his battles with the

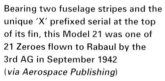

**Bearing two fuselage stripes and the unique 'X' prefixed serial at the top of its fin, this Model 21 was one of 21 Zeroes flown to Rabaul by the 3rd AG in September 1942 (*via Aerospace Publishing*)**

Grumman F6F Hellcat because he respected its fighting abilities; 'They were fast and manoeuvrable, and their pilots were good. They'd get on your tail and shower you with bullets! It was awful!'

Allied fighters slowly whittled down the JNAF at Rabaul to the point where the 20th AG had only one operational Zero left by 17 February 1944. When US carrier aircraft attacked the Japanese naval bastion at Truk and destroyed most of the island's fighters on the ground, orders were given to evacuate all airworthy machines immediately to Truk. By 25 February all that was left on Rabaul were a dozen 'junked' Zeroes which could not make the exodus and a few seaplanes. Rabaul would be bypassed by the Allied forces and allowed to 'wither on the vine'.

## Warrant Officer Satoshi Yoshino

A beneficiary of high quality pre-war flight training, Satoshi Yoshino would make full of this instruction during the Pacific War. Born in February 1918 in Chiba Prefecture, he was accepted into the naval flight reserve's enlisted pilot training course at 16 and graduated in August 1937. More tuition followed until March 1938, when Yoshino joined the first of several mainland air groups before being posted to the *Soryu* for active duty. He later became a member of the newly-organised Chitose AG, and in October 1941 advanced to the Marshall Islands with the group. Four months later Yoshino transferred to the 4th AG at Rabaul.

On 11 February 1942 he and three comrades in obsolete Type 96 'Claudes' caught three RAAF Hudsons over Gasmata, New Britain, and downed two – on the 13th he claimed another kill in the same area.

As part of the nucleus of veteran pilots in the 4th AG, Yoshino participated in heavy battles over Port Moresby and Horn Island, and by the time he joined the Tainan AG he had been promoted to warrant officer.

On 9 June 1942 Yoshino and his comrades scrambled to repel bombers heading for Lae. One group intercepted the 'heavies' while others engaged P-400s of the 39th FS, and it was one of the latter (flown by future P-38 ace 1/Lt Curran L Jones) which downed Yoshino near Cape Ward Hunt. The fallen ace duly received a posthumous promotion to ensign.

In 1988, Zero ace Saburo Sakai (Yoshino's comrade) met Curran 'Jack' Jones at a symposium in Fredericksburg, Texas, telling him, 'You must have been a great pilot yourself to have downed my comrade – Yoshino was one of our most outstanding pilots'.

According to Tainan AG records, Satoshi Yoshino achieved 15 kills.

## Ensign Saburo Sakai

As Japan's most famous Zero fighter ace, Saburo Sakai claims that his greatest wartime success was not scoring 60+ kills, but having never lost a wingman in over 200 dogfights. Born to a poor farming family in Saga Prefecture in 1916, the son of a Samurai joined the navy in May 1933 in order to escape the shame of having failed at school.

While serving aboard the battleship *Kirishima* as a sailor, Sakai became fascinated with aircraft and decided to become a pilot. After failing the entrance examination twice, he passed on his third attempt and was

WO Satoshi Yoshino entered flight training as a 16-year-old, and although he only lasted five months in combat over Rabaul and New Guinea, he achieved 15 victories (*Y Izawa*)

The first long-range mission flown from Rabaul to Guadalcanal on 7 August 1942 nearly cost the life of CPO Saburo Sakai. Given up for dead, he is shown here just minutes after landing making his way to headquarters to give his report. Sakai received shrapnel wounds to his face (the wounds to his eyes were so severe that he eventually lost the sight in his right one), chest, left leg and elbow (*Sakai/Maru*)

accepted into flight training. In November 1937 Sakai graduated at the top of his class, being awarded the Emperor's silver watch.

As a member of the 12th AG, he saw action in the China War, achieving his first aerial victory on his first combat mission on 5 October 1938. Sakai was at the controls of one of fifteen 'Claudes' bounced by I-16s during a mission to Hankow, and in the subsequent engagement he broke almost every rule in the book and was nearly killed. Sakai eventually shot down an enemy aircraft by using up his entire ammunition supply, and upon his return to base the young neophyte was severely chastised, rather than congratulated, by his commander for his inferior performance.

By 3 October 1939 PO2/c Sakai had become a seasoned pilot, and on this date he proved it by chasing down 12 DB-3 bombers that had raided Hankow Airfield in a surprise attack. Although slightly wounded, Sakai jumped into his 'Claude' and took off alone in hot pursuit. The running gunfight ranged over 150 miles, and culminated in the demise of one of the bombers. News of his daring assault preceded him back to Japan, and Sakai returned home to a hero's welcome.

In June 1941 PO1/c Sakai was posted to the Tainan AG, with whom he participated in the raid on Clark Field, in the Philippines, on the first day of the Pacific War. He destroyed two B-17s on the ground and claimed

Lt(jg) Junichi Sasai wore this silver belt buckle for good luck. It was made by his father and presented to him when he went off to war. Japanese legend says that the tiger will roam over a thousand miles on its hunt, but will always return home safely. Sasai presented this to the wounded Saburo Sakai, who was being shipped home for hospitalisation. About two weeks later Sasai failed to return from a mission to Guadalcanal (*Sakaida*)

Sakai's torn leather helmet and silk scarf bears testimony to his fierce encounter with SBD gunners on 7 August 1942. A .30 cal tracer bullet missed his right eye by inches, leaving its mark on the goggles, whilst bullet fragments shattered the lens and left him permanently blind in that eye. Sakai stuffed his silk scarf under his flying helmet to stop the bleeding (*Sakaida*)

one P-40 shot down, although the latter type, flown by Sam Grashio, managed escaped with a big cannon hole in its wing.

On 10 December Sakai engaged a B-17C of the 14th Bombardment Squadron in the air for the first time, which he duly downed, the Japanese pilot being both shocked by the sheer size of the Flying Fortress.

With the Philippines captured, the Tainan AG commenced operations in the Dutch East Indies, where Sakai once again battled the B-17;

'There was no weakest area of the B-17. Every time was a close call. A particular incident I remember was in February 1942 over Balikpapan, Borneo, before I developed any method of attacking the bomber. There were two Zeroes and seven B-17s. I did everything I could to kill this aircraft but was not successful. Nothing worked!'

On 28 February 1942 Sakai encountered a DC-3 transport while on a lone patrol mission east of Surabaya, Java. Pacing the aircraft, when he pulled alongside to inspect it before shooting it down he noticed a blonde-haired woman and a small child peering at him through a fuselage window – Sakai spared the transport, letting it go on its way.

In April 1942 the Tainan AG was transferred to Rabaul, Zero pilots rotating between here and Lae during the fight with American and Australian units based at Port Moresby.

Sakai also conducted a personal war against the officer class, who regarded the enlisted pilots as expendable. As a result, his men were fed monotonous meals and denied tobacco, so he ordered his wingman to steal from the officers' mess and gave his approval for his men to smoke in direct violation of orders. Faced with discipline and morale problems, the CO of the group eventually ordered that improvements be made.

As the senior pilot in the Sasai Squadron, Sakai tutored his comrades (including the unit's CO, Lt(jg) Junichi Sasai) in the art of dogfighting. Many of his pupils went on to become aces.

On 22 July 1942 eight Zeroes intercepted a lone RAAF Hudson (A16-201 of No 32 Sqn) whilst flying a fighter cover mission over Buna. Anticipating an easy kill, Sakai chased after the twin-engined bomber, whose pilot, Plt Off Warren F Cowan, whipped his aircraft around and made a head-on attack at Sakai. Outnumbered eight-to-one, Cowan remained on the offensive, scattering the Zeroes into wild disorder, before Sakai eventually shot him down. As the only living eyewitness to this action, Sakai wrote a testimonial to the Australian Defence Minister in 1997, requesting that Cowan and his crew be cited for bravery. It was denied.

On 7 August 1942, during the first long-range mission to Guadalcanal, PO1/c Sakai shot down a Wildcat flown by future ace Lt J J Southerland (see Osprey *Aircraft of the Aces 3 - Wildcat Aces of World War 2* for further details) of VF-5, who parachuted to safety. As Sakai rejoined his flight, he was ambushed by a lone SBD flown by Lt Dudley H Adams of VS-71, the American pilot succeeding in firing a bullet through the cockpit of the Zero, which just missed the startled pilot's head by inches. Stung into action, Sakai downed the Dauntless, killing tail-gunner Harry E Elliot in the process. Lt Adams managed to parachute to safety, however, and was subsequently awarded the Navy Cross.

Having despatched two aircraft already on this mission, Sakai spotted what he thought were eight Wildcats in the distance – they were, in fact, SBD dive-bombers of VB-6, led by Lt Carl Horenburger. Unaware that he had been spotted, Sakai raced in for the kill, only to find himself in a trap as the tail-gunners opened up with their twin .30 guns, severely wounding the JNAF ace. In an epic four-and-a-half hour flight, Sakai returned to base after having been given up for dead. Permanently blinded in one eye, he sent back to Japan for further hospitalisation.

Upon recovery, Sakai frustratingly found himself in the role of instructor, teaching an ever-shrinking training syllabus to larger and larger classes of increasingly more youthful pilots.

In June 1944, he was at last thrust back into frontline flying, being ordered to Iwo Jima to join the Yokosuka AG. On 24 June he engaged in a wild combat with Hellcats of VF-1, -2 and -50, claiming three destroyed. However, his unit lost a staggering 23 Zeroes in reply.

With no hope of turning the tide against the invading Americans, the Yokosuka AG was ordered to resort to *kamikaze* suicide attacks. On 5 July Sakai duly set out with two wingmen on a one-way mission, nine Zeroes escorting eight torpedo-bombers on a futile sortie. Before they could reach the target, they were bounced by Hellcats, and disobeying orders to refuse combat and stay with the bombers, Sakai fought back and downed a Hellcat. Despite the efforts of the escorts, all the torpedo-bombers were swiftly destroyed. leaving Sakai and his two charges to battle darkness, bad weather and low fuel states in their struggle to return to base.

Twenty-four hours later Sakai and the remaining Zero pilots evacuated back to Japan, where he returned to instructing due to his lack of a further combat assignment. Transferred to the 343rd AG in December 1944, Sakai trained pilots destined for the new Shiden-Kai 'George'.

The great ace's last combat occurred on 17 August 1945 when (two days after the surrender announcement) he sortied with other pilots of the Yokosuka AG against a B-32 Dominator sent to photo-recce Tokyo. By his reckoning, he destroyed or damaged over 60 aircraft during his career.

In 1982 Saburo Sakai shook hands with Harold L Jones, one of the SBD gunners who wounded him. A resident of Tokyo, he occasionally gives motivational lectures, and continues to write books. Although blind in his right eye, Sakai has achieved three 'holes-in-one' playing golf!

## Chief Petty Officer Sadao Uehara

Sadao Uehara was one of Saburo Sakai's original wingmen from the early days of the war. He entered flight training in June 1938 and graduated in October 1941, being immediately posted to the Tainan AG.

The opening day of the Pacific War saw Uehara flying against airfield targets at Luzon, in the Philippines, and on 19 February 1942 the young novice claimed his first victory when he shot down a P-40 of the 17th PS.

Uehara was one of the few original Tainan AG pilots to survive through to November 1942, when the unit was reorganised. By the time he returned to Japan, the following victories were recorded in his logbook; three P-40s, four F4Fs and a single P-39, TBF and B-25 (unconfirmed) – he also shared in the destruction of two B-17s, a PBY a C-47 and a Spitfire. After the disaster at Midway, many veteran pilots were pulled out of frontline duty to become instructors, Uehara included, and and like most of those affected by this decision, he hated his new assignment.

In September 1944, in anticipation of the American invasion of the

Pilots of the Tainan AG pose for the newspapers back home on 9 June 1942. In the front row, from left to right, are ; PO3/c Sadao Uehara, unidentified, Seaman 1/c Kenichiro Yamamoto and PO3/c Keisaku Yoshimura. Standing, left to right, are; PO1/c Saburo Sakai, PO3/c Seiji Ishikawa, war correspondent Hajime Yoshida and unidentified. Seconds after this photo was taken an air raid alarm sounded and the pilots scurried off into action (*Maru*)

Tainan AG 2nd Squadron pilots are seen at Rabaul in 1942. In the front row, from left to right, are; PO3/c Yoshizo Ohashi, PO3/c Seiji Ishikawa (5 victories), PO3/c Kenichi Kumagai (2 victories), Seaman 1/c Kenichiro Yamamoto and PO2/c Shin Nakano. In the second row, left to right, are; PO2/c Toshio Ota (34 victories), PO1/c Saburo Sakai (60+ victories), Seaman 1/c Masayoshi Yonekawa (6 victories) and PO3/c Unichi Miya. Standing, from left to right, are; PO1/c Hiroyoshi Nishizawa (86 victories), PO3/c Daizo Fukumori, PO3/c Yutaka Kimura, PO3/c Masuaki Endo (14 victories), PO1/c Katsumi Kobayashi and PO3/c Takeichi Kokubu. Of the pilots featured in these two group photographs, only Sakai, Uehara and Ishikawa survived the war (*Sakaida*)

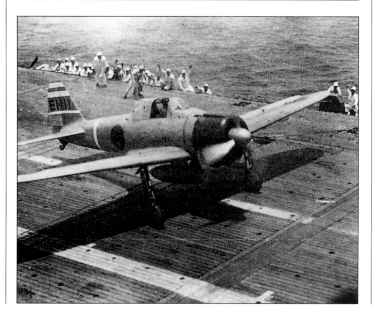

Lt Hideki Shingo sorties from the carrier *Shokaku* in October 1942 during the Battle of Santa Cruz. He was the squadron leader of the carrier's Zero fighters, and a most capable leader who had seen action during both the China War and the early campaigns of the Pacific War. Shingo eventually rose to lieutenant commander rank (*via Aerospace Publishing*)

A6M2-N floatplane fighters are seen under inspection by mechanics aboard the seaplane tender *Kamikawa Maru* in August 1942 – the ship was en route from Yokosuka to the Shortland Islands, in the Solomons. On 13 September WO Kawamura became the first pilot within the unit to score a victory when he engaged an SBD dive-bomber preparing to land at Henderson Field, on Guadalcanal. The 'Rufes' also frequently engaged B-17s over the Solomons (*Maru*)

Two 'Rufes' are seen on a training flight off the Japanese coastline in late 1942. The floatplanes initially entered service in the standard Zero fighter light grey scheme, although this was soon replaced by the drab green seen on the aircraft in the background

Philippines, the newly-reformed 201st AG (II) was activated at Davao. By this stage in the war the need for veteran pilots had reached such an acute level that even instructors were brought back for active combat duty, Sadao Uehara being duly transferred to the 306th Sqn of the 201st AG. He claimed his last victory (a F6F Hellcat) within days of joining the unit, but soon fell seriously ill in the tropical environment and was sent

back to Japan in December. CPO Uehara ended the war as an instructor.

By his own reckoning, he destroyed over 13 aircraft during the war. About three years after VJ-Day, he told his old flight leader, Saburo Sakai, 'I hated you for being so severe to me in the early days. But thanks to you, I survived the war!' Uehara became an accomplished helicopter pilot after the war. He was killed in a helicopter accident on 27 August 1988.

Mitsubishi F1M 'Pete' observation seaplanes are seen moored at their coastal base on Shortland Islands. The F1M was extremely manoeuvrable, and carried two forward firing 7.7 mm machine-guns plus a flexible weapon of the same calibre for the observer. The 'Pete' could also be armed with two 60 kg bombs under the wings (*Maru*)

## Warrant Officer Sadamu Komachi

Standing over six feet tall, Sadamu Komachi was one of the tallest Zero pilots in the JNAF, his daredevil skills and exploits being frequently chronicled in his prefecture's newspapers, which made him famous.

He was born in Ishikawa Prefecture in April 1920, and enlisted in the navy after turning 18. Komachi commenced his career as a fighter pilot

A pair of F1Ms carry out a coastal patrol. The heavy weathering of the aircraft's central float indicates just how much use this 'Pete' has seen (*via Phil Jarrett*)

after graduating from flight school in June 1940, his first assignment seeing him serve aboard the carrier *Shokaku*. On the opening day of the Pacific War he flew as protective cover over the Pearl Harbor attack fleet.

During the Battle of the Coral Sea in May 1942, Komachi recorded his first victories when he claimed two F4F Wildcats (one shared) and a dive-bomber. It was a Wildcat which also came close to nearly killing him on 24 August when he fought against F4Fs of VF-6 over Guadalcanal during the Battle of the Eastern Solomons. Spotting his prey below him, he dived down to make his kill. However, another Wildcat flown by Lt Albert Vorse quickly latched onto Komachi's tail and opened fire. Caught by surprise, the JNAF pilot feigned death by putting his Zero into a wild uncontrollable spin for 6000 ft. Vorse was so convinced by this desperate manoeuvre that he claimed a victory (his fifth out of an eventual tally of 11.5) and Komachi managed to cheat death.

During this combat much precious fuel had been consumed, and on his way back to base Komachi tanks ran dry and he was forced to ditch. He resigned himself to death while clinging to a floating drop tank, but a destroyer plucked him from the water at night using searchlights.

Rabaul – known as the 'Graveyard of Fighter Pilots' – was Komachi's next battle assignment, flying briefly with the 204th AG before transferring to the 253rd at Tobera airfield. Whilst here he became a specialist in the use of the aerial burst bomb (Ta-Dan) against formations of B-24s.

On the night of 18/19 February 1944, Rabaul and neighbouring areas were attacked by five American destroyers (*Farenholt*, *Buchanan*, *Lansdowne*, *Lardner* and *Woodworth)* of DesRon (Destroyer Squadron) 12. In column formation, they shelled various targets and launched 15 torpedoes against ships docked in Keravia Bay. Rabaul's coastal guns, designed for short distance firing only in anticipation of enemy landing attempts, remained silent, so PO1/c Komachi, livid with anger at their inability to fight back, volunteered to attack the enemy.

A single Zero, armed with two 60 kg bombs, roared off into the night. Purple flashes off the coast pinpointed the American destroyer convoy, whilst fires started by the vessels' shelling could be seen up and down the coast. Off Kokopo, the daring Zero pilot commenced his strafing attacks, which remained unchallenged by the ships. It was only when Komachi dropped his bombs (which missed) did the destroyers' anti-aircraft batteries responded fiercely. Komachi made repeated strafing attacks, then headed for home after exhausting his ammunition supply. He made the following report, 'I attacked the destroyers and set small to medium fires on three of them. I chased them out of the bay'. In reality the vessels had suffered very little damage, for the fires he had seen on the destroyers were actually the canvas gun covers burning away – in their haste to fire back, the ships' gunners had simply fired through the 'tarps'!

When the main element of the 253rd AG was withdrawn north to Truk on 19 February 1944, Komachi went with them and continued his struggle against the B-24s using aerial burst bombs from the island base. At this time he received the rare honour of a commendation from his superiors for his technical skills.

On 19 June 1944 15 Zeroes under the command of Lt Cdr Harutoshi Okamoto left Truk for Guam, in the Marianas. Unknown to the Zero pilots, who were running short of fuel, the airfield at Orote had just been

PO3/c Sadamu Komachi poses aboard the carrier *Shokaku* in early 1942. His exploits were well publicised in his home prefecture newspapers, and he gained a reputation for being a daring pilot (*K Osuo*)

raided by US carrier aircraft. The incoming flight of Zeroes was seen by the departing F6Fs, which quickly turned around and attacked at low altitude. In a head-on encounter with Ens Wendell Twelves of VF-15 at less than 200 ft, Komachi was caught off guard and his Zero took hits in the engine. Skilfully ditching his burning aircraft into the sea, he suffered serious burns to his face and body, but managed to swim ashore and eventually return to Japan by submarine – Komachi's Zero was one of two shot down Ens Twelves, these being his first kills. The Hellcat pilot would go one to score a further 11 victories (see Osprey *Aircraft of the Aces 10 - Hellcat Aces of World War 2* for further details).

Back in Japan, Komachi served with the Yokosuka AG until the end of the war . . . and a few days beyond. On 18 August 1945 he participated in the second interception of B-32 Dominators of the 386th Bomb Squadron over Tokyo, damaging the aircraft flown by Lt John R Anderson. Although the attack on the B-32s was legal under international law (Japan was still technically at war until the official surrender documents were signed on 2 September 1945), Komachi was fearful of Allied reprisals, and went 'underground' until US Occupation Forces left his country.

WO Sadamu Komachi flew around 2500 hours during World War 2, during which time he engaged in over 180 dogfights, force-landed twice and was shot down once. Attributed with over 40 kills by his peers, Komachi reckons that he scored 'perhaps half' of this total.

In 1994 he corresponded with Wendell Twelves of Springville, Utah, and they had plans to meet, but the pilot who downed Komachi during the 'Marianas Turkey Shoot' sadly passed away after a heart operation. Two years earlier the JNAF ace had been a guest panelist at the Battle of the Coral Sea Symposium at NAS Pensacola, Florida. He remarked, 'I'm just a lowly warrant officer, but I had admirals and captains saluting me and shaking my hand. This would never happen in Japan!'

## Warrant Officer Gitaro Miyazaki

Gitaro Miyazaki was one of many Tainan AG aces who distinguished themselves over New Guinea in 1942. Born in June 1917 in Kochi Prefecture, he entered navy flight training in May 1933 and graduated in May 1937. Miyazaki subsequently served with the Saiki and Takao AGs.

In September 1938 (whilst flying with the 12th AG) Miyazaki was posted to the China War, although by the time he arrived in-theatre Chinese aerial opposition had begun to waver, and it wasn't until 5 October that he achieved his first victory – an I-16 over Hankow. He returned to Japan in June 1939 and joined the Yokosuka AG, although he was posted back to China for a second tour of duty with the 12th AG in 1941. Miyazaki claimed another victory on 11 August over Chengtu.

Following the organisation of the Tainan AG on the island of Formosa in October 1941, Miyazaki was posted to the unit as a newly-promoted warrant officer. On the opening day of the Pacific War, he was a flight leader in the 3rd Squadron which attacked Clark Field, in the Philippines, claiming one victory during the course of the mission.

Still with the Tainan AG, Miyazaki sortied over the Dutch East Indies before arriving at Rabaul in April 1942. From here He flew combat patrol missions against the enemy airfield at Port Moresby. On 1 June 24 P-39s

WO Gitaro Miyazaki's devotion to duty cost him his life, comrade Saburo Sakai, who witnessed his demise, blaming his death on ill health and a lack of teamwork (*Y Izawa*)

and P-400s of the USAAF 35th and 36th FSs (on the last day of their combat tours) scrambled to oppose an incoming flight of 24 'Betty' bombers escorted by a dozen Zeroes. The Americans tore into the bombers while the fighter escorts tried desperately to repel their attacks, and as the bombers completed their runs and turned for home, Miyazaki, who was below the 'Bettys', was viciously attack by an enemy aircraft that had dived straight through the formation at him. Hit repeatedly by cannon and machine gun fire, the Zero exploded in mid-air, killing its pilot.

Miyazaki was awarded a rare posthumous double rank promotion to lieutenant (junior grade) after his death. His tally of 13 kills was officially recognised, and the Naval All Units Proclamation No 3 stated that he had flown 37 missions and his flight had accounted for 44 aircraft destroyed, six burned on the ground and 30+ damaged. Miyazaki was the third of ten Tainan AG pilots honoured with posthumous double promotions.

## Petty Officer Third Class Toshiaki Honda

Saburo Sakai's faithful wingman, Toshiaki Honda was also a character within the Tainan AG when out of the cockpit, his antics bringing comic relief to his comrades in the miserable environment of the tropics. He was born in Fukuoka Prefecture in 1919, and prior to his enlistment in the navy, he had worked as a ticket collector on a city tram.

Honda was accepted for flight training and graduated in June 1940. He became a member of the Tainan AG and flew his first combat mission during the attack against Clark Field on 8 December 1941 as the third man in the flight of Saburo Sakai and Ichio Yokogawa. Tangling with P-40s of the 21st Pursuit Squadron over the airfield, Honda failed to score.

After the assault on the Philippines, the Tainan AG ranged over the Dutch East Indies, then proceeded to the forward base at Rabaul. Once here, the group alternated between Rabaul and Lae. While at the latter airfield pilot morale sharply declined due to both the poor quality of meals and inequities between officers and enlisted pilots. Honda, who had a reputation as a scrounger, was duly ordered by Sakai to pillage the officers' mess kitchen for food to bring back to his squadronmates. Success in his task soon led to carelessness, as Honda was caught and beaten by an irate officer, who only stopped when Sakai fired his pistol at him – a court martial offence. Summoned before Cdr Yasuna Kozono, Sakai explained his actions and his mens' complaint, and astonishingly the incident was 'forgotten about' and the cuisine dramatically improved!

While Honda was not a gifted pilot, he was quite aggressive, and on 17 April 1942 he claimed three P-40s shot down over Port Moresby. He always told others, 'As long as I fly with Sakai, I'll never be shot down!'

On 13 May newcomer to the unit WO Watari Handa (see China War chapter) requested the loan of Honda from Sakai for a sweep over the airfield at Port Moresby. Despite Honda's protestation, Sakai ordered his wingman to go, and the Zero flight was duly bounced by seven P-39s of the 36th FS over the target. Capt Paul G Brown and 1Lt Elmer F Ghram caught Honda in a crossfire and the Zero exploded, killing the pilot.

Due to his fighting spirit, Toshiaki Honda was given a rare two rank posthumous promotion to petty officer first class, his citation stating that he had flown 47 missions, achieved five personal kills and 18 assists.

PO3/c Toshiaki Honda was the best wingman Saburo Sakai ever had, and also the most mischievous – Sakai grew suspicious of his wingman's endless supply of clean underwear, only to discover that Honda was stealing his! When confronted by Sakai, Honda admitted to the dastardly deed. The former later ordered him to steal food from the officer's mess (*Maru*)

## Petty Officer First Class Masuaki Endo

For those Zero pilots who fought through the tough combats over New Guinea and Guadalcanal in 1942, the invaluable experience gained in battle only served to make them better pilots. Masuaki Endo was one of the few veterans from the Tainan AG to have survived these epic battles.

Born in Fukushima Prefecture in December 1920, Endo enlisted in the navy and graduated from flight training in October 1941. In February of the following year he was posted to the Tainan AG, advancing with it to Rabaul and Lae. A consistent scorer throughout the early months of war, Endo seemingly led a charmed life as his comrades fell one by one.

On 7 August 1942 the group flew the first long-range mission to Guadalcanal from its base at Rabaul – a one-way distance of over 560 miles. Seventeen Zeroes escorted twenty-seven 'Betty' bombers to counterattack the American landings on Guadalcanal, PO2/c Endo flying as second wingman to Lt(jg) Junichi Sasai. In his first combat with carrier fighters, the 21-year-old ace claimed an F4F and a pair of SBDs.

Subsequent missions to Guadalcanal took a heavy toll of veteran pilots, but Endo still cheated death through a combination of his flying skill and luck. In November 1942 the few surviving pilots were ordered back to Japan while the unit was reorganised as the 251st AG.

In May 1943 Endo returned to Rabaul as a member of the 251st, but failed to survive his first month back in action. On 7 June, the Japanese sortied 81 Zeroes and clashed with over 100 American and New Zealand fighters over the Russells. PO2/c Endo reportedly downed a P-38 (none were lost) before his aircraft was set on fire following a head-on attack by a P-40 flown by Lt Henry E Matson of the 44th FS. Determined to take his foe with him, Endo rammed his flaming Zero into the Warhawk, Matson parachuted out at 18,000 ft with burns to his face, neck and hands, and a mouthful of powdered Plexiglas. Endo was killed. Subsequently rescued, Matson was duly credited with two A6Ms destroyed.

Masuaki Endo received official recognition for 14 victories.

## Lieutenant(jg) Junichi Sasai

Junichi Sasai earned the title 'Richthofen of Rabaul', and despite seeing combat for only a short period of time, his legacy as a great fighter-leader lives on to this day.

Born on 13 February 1918 in Tokyo as the son of a naval captain, young Junichi was always destined join the service as an officer when he reached an appropriate age. His early childhood was marked by ill health, resulting in him often being absent from school and teasing by his classmates. A regime of hard physical exercise and diet improved the youngster's health, however, and by the time he enrolled in high school, Junichi was fit enough to earn his Blackbelt in Judo – his outstanding achievements in school won him acceptance to Etajima (Naval Academy).

Sasai graduated in 1939 and was commissioned an ensign. He entered flight training and completed the course in November 1941, his tenacious spirit earned him the nickname of 'Gamecock'. By the time Japan entered the Pacific War the following month, Sasai had joined the Tainan AG. He flew with the group on a raid to Luzon (in the Philippines) on 10

PO3/c Masuaki Endo on 4 August 1942 at Rabaul. He was one of the few Tainan AG pilots to survive its first combat tour, which ended in November 1942. He returned from Japan to the Solomons in May 1943, but lasted barely a month before being killed (*Y Izawa*)

December, but he experienced engine trouble and was forced to abort.

Following victory in the Philippines, the Tainan AG saw considerable action in the Dutch East Indies, where it provided air support for ground troops. Sasai's first victory was recorded on 2 February 1942 over Maospati, Java, when he destroyed a Dutch Buffalo. Sixteen days later he claimed a P-40E of the 17th PS with just 280 rounds of machine-gun fire.

The Tainan AG advanced to Rabaul in April 1942, being reorganised with new officers, equipment and pilots soon after its arrival. Lt(jg) Sasai was duly given command of the 2nd Squadron, and pilots alternated between Rabaul and their forward base at Lae.

Within 2nd Squadron ranks were many experienced enlisted pilots, including PO1/c Saburo Sakai. The latter was most impressed with his new commander, for he showed genuine compassion towards his men unlike other officers. To insure his survival, Sakai personally tutored the young lieutenant in the art of dogfighting, and once Sasai found his shooting eye, he blossomed into a first rate pilot.

On 4 May 1942 he demonstrated his marksmanship by bouncing a flight of three P-39s and shooting them all down in less than 20 seconds. Sasai continued to score multiple victories, achieving his personal best of five in one day on 7 August 1942 over Guadalcanal. This feat was tempered by the serious wounding of his mentor Saburo Sakai during the same mission, and before the latter was sent back to Japan, Sasai gave him a personal memento – his special tiger belt buckle – which he claimed would protect him from further harm.

On 26 August Sasai led a nine-aircraft formation tasked with protecting 'Betty' bombers sent to strike at Henderson Field, on Guadalcanal. They were attacked over the target by 12 Wildcats from VMF-223, led by Majs John L Smith and Rivers J Morrell. Sasai failed to return from the mission.

In a letter to his family prior to his death, Sasai claimed 54 victories, and stated that he hoped to break the record of German World War 1 ace, Baron Manfred von Richthofen (who achieved 80 kills). According to the Naval All Units Proclamation No36, Sasai flew 76 missions with the Tainan AG and attained 27 recognised victories. He was promoted two grades to lieutenant commander for distinguished service.

## Petty Officer First Class Toshio Ota

Toshio Ota belonged to the 'Clean Up Trio' in the Tainan AG, which was the premier JNAF unit operating against the Allies in New Guinea. The remaining trio members were Saburo Sakai and Hiroyoshi Nishizawa, who were two of the top aces in the air group at the time.

Ota was born in March 1919 to a farming family in Nagasaki Prefecture, and as a youth he was enthused with aviation and joined the navy at Sasebo in 1936. He was accepted into flight training in January 1939 and graduated in September. The China War was by then in its second year, and the exploits of JNAF pilots had received considerable newspaper coverage at home. Anxious for action, Ota passed through the Omura and 12th Air Groups before heading to China in June 1941. However, by the time he arrived in-theatre the air action had diminished considerably and he saw no combat.

Dubbed the 'Richthofen of Rabaul', Lt(jg) Junichi Sasai was a compassionate officer who treated his enlisted men with respect, unlike most of the officer pilots at Rabaul (*S Sakai*)

PO1/c Toshio Ota was the leader of the scoring race within the Tainan AG in 1942. Popular within his squadron because of his congenial ways, Ota nevertheless exhibited tremendous fighting spirit once in the air (*Sakaida*)

With the outbreak of the Pacific War, Ota flew as a member in the 3rd Squadron of the Tainan AG in the aerial assault on Clark Field on 8 December 1941, claiming one aircraft shot down. After this action, he sortied to the Dutch East Indies, where he was wounded over Balikpapan, Borneo, in a running gunfight with a B-17 – Ota was subsequently grounded for a number of months because of his wounds.

The Tainan AG was ordered to their new base at Rabaul in April 1942, Ota being transferred to Lt(jg) Junichi Sasai's 2nd Squadron upon arrival. He soon made a name for himself by doggedly pursuing a lone B-17 for over an hour before finally bringing it down.

Ota's congenial personality and aggressive fighting spirit soon caught the attention of Saburo Sakai (the unit's top scorer), and as with Lt(jg) Sasai, Sakai also tutored the former in dogfighting techniques. His protégé caught on very quickly, and soon a scoring race had developed between himself, his instructor and Hiroyoshi Nishizawa. Ota proved his ability on the 7 August mission to Guadalcanal, when he claimed four Wildcats destroyed in his first encounter with American carrier fighters.

On 21 October PO1/c Toshio Ota participated in a bomber escort mission to Guadalcanal which encountered Wildcats of VMF-212 head-on at high altitude. Although Ota quickly downed Marine Gunner 'Tex' Hamilton (a seven-kill ace), who parachuted out but was never recovered, he in turn had 1Lt Frank C Drury (six kills) whip around onto his tail in a tight climbing turn as the Zero flashed before him. The Wildcat pilot's aim was deadly accurate, and Ota fell to his death – Drury claimed two A6Ms during this sortie.

Toshio Ota was given a posthumous promotion to the rank of warrant officer, and according to his air group's record, he had scored 34 victories.

## Warrant Officer Hiroyoshi Nishizawa

It was only after his death that Hiroyoshi Nishizawa rose to fame, thanks to the memoir of his comrade Saburo Sakai. Indeed, he was at one time thought to have been the JNAF's top ace.

Born on 27 January 1920 in Nagano Prefecture, Nishizawa was the son of a saké brewery manager. He joined the navy in June 1936 as a result of seeing a JNAF recruiting poster, the youngster working in a thread mill at the time. His boyhood dream of becoming a pilot was realised when he completed flying training in March 1939.

When the Pacific War began, Nishizawa was flying Type 96 'Claudes' with the Chitose AG in the Marshall Islands, and he duly accompanied the group to Rabaul, where he joined the 4th AG in February 1942. Nishizawa recorded his first victory on 3 February 1942 over Rabaul whilst still flying the thoroughly obsolete 'Claude'.

When elements of the Tainan AG arrived at Rabaul from the Dutch East Indies in April, Nishizawa was transferred into the 2nd Squadron, where he found himself in the company of PO1/c Saburo Sakai. The latter tutored the gaunt and sickly loner, together with PO2/c Toshio Ota, and together the threesome became famous as the 'Cleanup Trio'.

Nishizawa quickly mastered the art of dogfighting, scoring his first victory (a P-39) with the Tainan AG on 1 May over Port Moresby. The following day two P-40s fell to his guns, the group's American opponents throughout the month of May being the USAAC's 35th and 36th FSs.

Nishizawa's most successful day came on 7 August 1942 when, during a long-range bomber escort mission to Guadalcanal, he claimed six VF-5 F4Fs in his first encounter with American carrier fighters. Although the great ace's A6M sustained some damage, he returned safely to base.

In November, surviving pilots of the Tainan AG were transferred to the 251st, with those few who had survived the combats over Guadalcanal being held in high esteem by the JNAF.

On 14 May 1943 33 Zeroes escorted 18 'Betty' bombers sent to strike at shipping in Oro Bay. Opposing them was the 49th FG, who scrambled up three squadrons of P-40s. In the huge dogfight which ensued, Nishizawa claimed one Warhawk shot down and two more as probables, plus recorded his first victory over a P-38 – the JNAF claimed 15 victories in total, but the only USAAF loss was a solitary P-38 (from the 9th FS).

It was inevitable that sooner or later Nishizawa would test his skills against the gull-winged F4U Corsair – arguably the best fighter on either side in the region. This contest occurred on 7 June 1943 over the Russells, when 81 Zeroes tangled with USMC and RNZAF fighters. Four Corsairs of VMF-112 were lost in this action, although three of the pilots were saved – Nishizawa's claims for the mission were one F4U and a New Zealand P-40 destroyed.

For the rest of the summer of 1943 he fought daily battles with Corsairs and P-40s in the areas of Rendova and Vella La Vella, the former fighter being his toughest opponent. Marines from VMF-121, -122, -123, -124 and -221 all traded fire with 'The Devil', but failed to bring him down, resulting in Nishizawa being awarded a coveted ceremonial sword from Adm Jinichi Kusaka, CO of the 11th Air Fleet.

In September the 251st AG was re-rolled as a nightfighter unit, and PO1/c Nishizawa was transferred to the 253rd AG, based at Tobera Airfield (Rabaul). He flew with his new unit for just a month, however, for he was ordered to return to Japan in October to serve as an instructor as part of the JNAF's efforts to cure their fighter pilot shortage. The following month he received promotion to warrant officer.

Nishizawa hated his new assignment likening it to baby-sitting. He had very little patience with his trainees, many of whom would have been rejected for flight training just three years earlier, and after repeated requests for a combat assignment, he was transferred to the 201st AG in the Philippines in time to participate in the counterattack against the American naval fleets.

The first successful *kamikaze* suicide attack occurred on 25 October 1944 when Lt Yukio Seki and four other pilots attacked US carriers in Leyte Gulf. WO Nishizawa had played a pivotal role in this mission by leading the four escort fighters which had cleared the path for Seki by downing two patrolling Hellcats. He subsequently told his comrades that he would die soon, and requested a *kamikaze* assignment, although this was swiftly turned down because of his value as a fighter pilot.

On 26 October Nishizawa boarded a bomber used by the Navy's 1021 Transport Group and left Cebu Island for Mabalacat (near Clark Field) to pick up some replacement Zeroes. A frantic SOS radio message was received from the transport, but it failed to arrive at its destination and nothing more was learned of its fate.

**PO1/c Hiroyoshi Nishizawa is seen as an instructor in Japan in 1943. He was not well suited to this task as he had very little tolerence for his trainees, and thus hating his assignment. Nishizawa was simply a skilled fighter pilot who could not teach (*K Osuo*)**

In 1982, the circumstances surrounding Nishizawa's death were finally resolved. The aircraft had been intercepted between Puerta Gallera and Calapan, on the northern tip of Mindoro Island, by two Hellcats from VF-14 that were in the process of returning to their carrier.

'I stayed below a thin stratus cloud layer and my wingman stayed on top', recalled F6F pilot Harold P Newell. 'The aircraft popped out of the clouds slightly to my right in a left hand turn. It was at close range and I opened fire. After several short bursts the port engine and inboard wing section were in flames. The aircraft went into an increasingly steep diving left turn and I continued firing until the fuselage started shedding pieces and the fire increased.'

Lt(jg) Harold P Newell received credit for shooting down the bomber, which he identified as a 'Helen' – a JAAF Ki-49 twin-engined bomber which, at this stage in the war, the JNAF sometimes used for transport duties. Nishizawa's aircraft was not a DC-3 as reported elsewhere.

Hiroyoshi Nishizawa was posthumously elevated two ranks to lieutenant junior grade and issued a citation. According to the Naval All Units Proclamation No 172, Nishizawa attained a personal tally of 36 victories and two damaged while serving with the 201st. Shortly before his death, Nishizawa had reportedly told his last CO, Cdr Harutoshi Okamoto, that he had achieved 86 kills – postwar, he has been linked with scores of 147 and 103, but both tallies are pure fiction.

In May 1982, Harold P Newell met and shook hands with Nishizawa's mentor, Saburo Sakai, at a reunion in California.

## Petty Officer Second Class Enji Kakimoto

Enji Kakimoto was typical of the many nameless Zero aces who enjoyed a brief career before been killed in the wholesale destruction of the JNAF. Officially listed as missing in action in August 1942, it wasn't until 1985 that his fate was finally unearthed.

He was born in Oita Prefecture in April 1920, and when the China War broke out in July 1937, he was so imbued with national spirit that he left his family farm and enlisted in the navy at Sasebo. The exploits of Japanese aviators over China excited young Enji, who initially served as a sailor aboard the cruiser *Myoko* following his enlistment. Once back ashore, he found that performing guard duty at various air bases was just as monotonous as farm labour, so he applied for, and was accepted into, flight training. He graduated in the 47th term flight class in October 1939.

Kakimoto's biggest day in action came during the fierce dogfight over Guadalcanal on 7 August 1942 when, as PO1/c Saburo Sakai's wingman, he claimed an F4F Wildcat and an SBD over Tulagi.

Just 20 days later PO2/c Kakimoto was shot down while escorting 'Val' dive-bombers on a mission to Rabi, New Guinea, ditching his Zero into the sea and swimming ashore. Captured by 'friendly' natives soon after reaching land, the young aviator was eventually turned over to the Australians. When Kakimoto failed to return from the mission he was declared missing and presumed killed in action.

Unbeknown to his squadron mates, Kakimoto had been shipped back to Australia, where he was imprisoned at the huge Cowra PoW camp in New South Wales. He played dumb with his captors, submitting to their

PO2/c Enji Kakimoto (seen here on 4 August 1942) was one of just a handful of Zero pilots who became a PoW. He helped organise the mass breakout from Cowra PoW Camp, in Australia, in 1944 (*Sakaida*)

questions and giving them misleading information. His fellow comrades remembered him as a militant hothead, who helped organise a breakout in a gesture aimed at erasing the shame of having been captured.

On 5 August 1944, more than 1100 Japanese PoWs broke out of the camp, and over 230 were either killed attempting to do so, or committed suicide rather than be recaptured – within nine days, all escapees had been accounted for. Although one of the main conspirators in the 'Cowra Breakout', Kakimoto never actually left the confines of the camp, choosing instead to throw a rope over a rafter in his hut and hang himself.

PO2/c Enji Kakimoto scored over five victories in his short career and now lies buried in the Japanese War Cemetery at Cowra.

## Ensign Kenji Okabe

Kenji Okabe is honoured in JNAF history as having been the pilot who initially set the record for the most number of victories achieved during one mission.

Born in Fukuoka Prefecture in May 1915, Kenji joined the Navy and entered flight training in the 38th term class along with fellow sailor Saburo Sakai. Upon graduation in November 1937, he was assigned to the 12th AG and went to the China War. However, there was very little enemy air activity to be found, and Okabe saw no combat. Unlike Sakai, he then became a carrier pilot and their careers took different paths.

When Japan attacked Pearl Harbor, PO1/c Okabe was assigned to the carrier *Shokaku*, although his part in the raid consisted of flying combat air patrols over the carrier task force. His baptism of fire finally came on 9 April 1942 when JNAF carrier pilots attacked the British naval base at Trincomalee, on the island of Ceylon (now Sri Lanka) – Okabe claimed the destruction two No 261 Sqn Hurricane IIs.

He subsequently made a name for himself during the Battle of the Coral Sea on 8 May 1942. During a combat air patrol over the *Shokaku*, Okabe attempted to thwart determined attack by SBDs against his carrier. Protecting the Dauntlesses were F4F Wildcats, which constantly interfered by drawing his flight into dogfights while the dive-bombers tried to deliver their bombs. SBD pilot Lt John J Powers managed to break through the fighter barrier to hit the carrier, causing extensive damage and put it out of action – he was killed in the process, however, later being posthumously awarded the Medal of Honor for his actions.

When the fighting ended Okabe claimed three SBDs and three F4Fs destroyed, with a further a pair of Wildcats as probables – a new JNAF record had been set. Despite his best efforts, Okabe's carrier had been so badly damaged that he was forced to ditch, from where he was rescued.

By July 1943 Okabe was back on his old ship, and in November the *Shokaku* Fighter Squadron flew to Rabaul to help shore up the flagging defense of the base in the face of relentless Allied air attacks. The Coral Sea veteran participated in a number of intercept missions whilst ashore, adding more victories to his tally.

Okabe's carrier fighter career ended when he transferred to the Omura AG in Japan. He fought briefly in the Philippines from October 1944 until he returned to Japan towards the end of the year, and then went on to see further action during aerial attacks over Okinawa in April 1945

PO3/c Kenji Okabe is seen in 1942 whilst serving aboard the *Shokaku*. He set a naval record of eight enemy aircraft destroyed in a day during the Battle of the Coral Sea (*Sakaida*)

PO1/c Kiyomi Katsuki became the second ranking JNAF floatplane ace of World War 2. He also saved the seaplane carrier *Nisshin* from certain destruction by destroying a B-17 in a ramming attack (*K Osuo*)

The three hatchets displayed over the unit code N1-118 on this A6M2-N seaplane fighter denote victories scored by the aircraft in the Solomons in 1942. Lt Keizo Yamazaki flew this aircraft with the 802nd AG, claiming a P-39 probable on 13 February 1943 (*K Osuo*)

with the 601st AG. After falling to halt the US invasion of Okinawa, Okabe's unit was all but grounded as it strove to conserve fuel and build up its aircraft inventory for the final battle which never came.

Ens Kenji Okabe claimed over 50 victories in his career.

## Warrant Officer Kiyomi Katsuki

The JNAF produced just two floatplane aces during World War 2, with Kiyomi Katsuki being one of them. Born in Fukuoka Prefecture in April 1919, he joined the navy in June 1938, and by May 1941 had graduated from flight training for the seaplane reconnaissance role – assignments to various units followed.

When the Pacific War started, Katsuki was flying from the seaplane tender *Chitose*, and he completed a number of reconnaissance and patrol missions over the Philippines and the Dutch East Indies in an F1M 'Pete' biplane scout. On 11 January 1942 the Japanese sent a convoy of special landing force marines to Kema, in the Northern Celebes, which was opposed by Seven Dutch and American PBYs off Menado. Katsuki and his squadronmates attacked the flying boats in their 'Petes', the former downing a Dutch PBY (No Y-58 of GVT-17) for his first victory.

In September 1942 Katsuki was transferred to a forward seaplane base in the Shortland Islands to undertake patrol missions to Guadalcanal. On 4 October, while flying combat air patrol over the fleet in his 'Pete', he spotted four enemy fighters and five B-17s. In order to prevent the the bombers from hitting the seaplane carrier *Nisshin*, Katsuki dove on the lead Flying Fortress – a B-17E of the 72nd BS, flown by Lt David C Everitt Jr – and commenced his attack. After completing his pass, he rammed the aircraft from below, tearing the right main wing and the vertical stabiliser off the bomber and damaging his own right wing. The gutsy pilot and his observer quickly baled out of their 'Pete' and were rescued by the destroyer *Akizuki*. The crew of the B-17 all perished.

For the actions of 4 October, in which Katsuki thwarted the bombing of the *Nisshin,* he received the following rare personal citation from Capt Tamotsu Furukawa, CO of the *Chitose*, which stated in part;

'Kiyomi Katsuki found four American fighters and five B-17s coming over the *Nisshin*. He started attacking the lead B-17; the return gunfire was very severe. But he had to stop this aircraft at all costs, so he decided to ram it. He approached from 50 metres under the B-17 and then turned just before contact, and tore off the main wing of the enemy bomber. His aircraft was broken up and he parachuted. Because of his attack, the enemy stopped attacking the fleet . . . In front of the enemy, you stayed calm and decided on the right method and did it. Your deed is most admirable. To attack the enemies at the risk of your own life is our Navy tradition . . . You are hereby awarded a special award of a gold chevron.'

Katsuki later returned to Japan and began conversion training from seaplane scout ('Pete') to seaplane fighter ('Rufe') at Yokusuka Air Base. He was then assigned to the 452nd AG and posted to their base at Shumshu, in the Aleutians, around July 1943. Soon after his arrival USAAF Eleventh Air Force B-25s and B-24s started pounding the Japanese on Paramushiru Island, in the frigid Kuriles, and eventually recaptured Attu Island in May. Between August and October Katsuki claimed a B-25.

On 12 September Maj Frank T Cash of the 404th BS led a flight of B-24s to attack a troop staging area on Paramushiru Island. Ten seaplanes teamed with JAAF 'Oscars' of the 54th Sentai to attack the Liberators, and Katsuki and four comrades duly claimed two B-24s destroyed – one of these was flown by Maj Cash.

PO3/c Katsuki and the few surviving members of his seaplane unit left the area when their seaplane base finally froze over, returning to Japan on board the submarine I-36. Upon arriving back at Yokosuka, he commenced conversion onto the new Kawanishi N1K Kyofu 'Rex' seaplane fighter. Upon completing his training, Katsuki was assigned to the 934th AG, moving with the group to Ambon Island in the south-west Pacific area of Indonesia. In January 1944 he used a 'Rex' to destroy a B-24, which was the type's first success, although this victory was one of the few

A mix of green and grey 'Rufes' of the 802nd AG are seen lined up at their Imieji base in the Marshall Islands on 27 May 1943. The second aircraft from the left is N1-118 (seen on the previous page in detail), flown by Lt Keizo Yamazaki. Seaplanes could make a base in any area of calm water, with tents providing shelter for pilots and mechanics alike (*Maru*)

Pilots and mechanics stand to attention awaiting inspection, again on the Marshall Islands
(*via Robert C Mikesh*)

A6M3a Zero 22s of the 251st AG are seen in a rare air-to-air photograph heading out on a patrol from Rabaul in 1943. The tail code of this fighter was originally UI-105, but at various times the prefix 'UI' was painted out with the hastily applied green daubed over the remainder of the aircraft's previously grey fuselage. This particular fighter was one of many flown by veteran ace Hiroyoshi Nishizawa, and it seen here carrying a 330 l (72.6 Imp gal) drop tank (*via Aerospace Publishing*)

high points for the group, which was disbanded shortly afterwards. The veteran seaplane pilot then undertook further conversion training to learn to fly the Zero fighter from land, and was subsequently posted to the 381st AG. He later flew in the defence of the Balikpapan oilfields, before downing a further two enemy aircraft over Singapore.

In February 1945, Katsuki returned to Japan and was based at Omura airfield, where he flew Raidens on home defence sorties until the surrender. His final tally of at least 16 kills included seven scored in seaplanes.

## Warrant Officer Kenji Yanagiya

Kenji Yanagiya would have been considered an 'average' Zero pilot but

VAdm Jinichi Kusaka (in the dark cap) was CO of the JNAF at Rabaul. He had previously headed the Naval Academy at Etajima prior to his appointment to the 11th Air Fleet in the South-east Pacific. Kusaka instituted the unofficial awarding of ceremonial swords to pilots for distinguished service, and he served at Rabaul from 1942 until the end of the war (*Maru*)

for fate, as he was the sole surviving escort pilot of the disastrous Adm Yamamoto mission.

Yanagiya was born in March 1919, and he enlisted in the navy as a seaman recruit in January 1940 at Yokosuka Naval Station. Subsequently plucked out of the ranks for flight training, he completed his course at Oita Air Base in March 1942 and was then assigned to the 6th AG.

In October 1942 Yanagiya was sent to Rabaul to serve with the 204th AG, and he recorded his first victory with the group on 5 January 1943 during an attack on Buin, on Bougainville, by P-38s (from the 339th FS) and B-17s. Although Yanagiya claimed a twin-engined Grumman XF5F-1 Skyrocket as his victim, this was an experimental fighter which never saw service – two P-38s were lost on this mission.

On 18 April Yanagiya, and five other pilots, was assigned to escort two 'Betty' bombers conducting an inspection tour of the frontlines – the lead bomber carried Adm Isoroku Yamamoto, Commander in Chief of the Combined Fleet. Sixteen P-38s from Guadalcanal intercepted the Japanese flight off the south-west coast of Bougainville, and Adm Yamamoto's bomber was shot down by 1Lt Rex Barber before the Japanese could take any effective action. The other 'Betty' was also destroyed.

In the ensuing dogfight, Yanagiya claimed one P-38, but it was to be a hollow victory. Having failed to protect their leader, yet having all returned to base unscathed, the escort pilots were given every opportunity to redeem themselves through glorious death – within three months four were dead.

On 8 June 1943 Yanagiya was severely wounded in combat while on a mission to Guadalcanal. His right arm was amputated and he was sent home to Japan for further hospitalisation.

By October of 1944 Yanagiya had recovered enough to become an instructor, but he never saw combat again. He ended the war with at least eight victories and married the nurse who had taken care of him.

In April 1988, Yanagiya shook hands with Rex Barber and the surviving P-38 veterans from the Yamamoto Mission at the Adm Nimitz Museum in Fredericksburg, Texas. He still lives in Tokyo today.

## Warrant Officer Hiroshi Okano

Although a late starter in the Tainan AG, Hiroshi Okano had risen to

Kenji Yanagiya was the sole wartime survivor of the Zero escorts assigned to protect Adm Yamamoto during his fateful frontline tour in April 1943. He was amazed by the celebrity status accorded to him for his role in the mission by American historians and veteran P-38 pilots alike when he visited the USA in 1988 (*Sakaida*)

PO3/c Hiroshi Okano scored six victories with the Tainan AG and a dozen more with the 201st AG in the Solomons. Of the 21 pilots in his training class, only he and two others survived the war (*Sakaida*)

A happy PO Sekizen Shibayama is seen in the cockpit of a 'Claude' whilst serving as a flying instructor. Posted to Rabaul in late 1943, he flew as part of the 'Guerrilla Air Force' after the JNAF had officially departed the area. Shibayama, and a handful of other pilots and mechanics, performed a commendable job in an impossible situation (*S Shibayama*)

prominence by the end of the war. Born in Ibaragi Prefecture in May 1921, he enlisted in the navy in June 1938. The start of the Pacific War found Okano flying in the Marshall Islands with the Chitose AG, although he was posted to the Tainan AG at Rabaul in late May 1942.

On 25 June, the Tainan AG sortied 25 Zeroes from Lae to attack Port Moresby. Along the way, they intercepted six B-17s escorted by 24 escort fighters, and in the wild dogfight that ensued, Okano claimed his first kill.

In December 1942 he was transferred to the 201st AG and returned once again to the Marshall Islands. There was no enemy air activity to be found in this region, however, and Okano's unit spent most of its time training and conducting patrols. In February 1943, the group was recalled to Japan, where the pilots underwent more training.

As the air war over the Solomons intensified, the 201st AG was rushed to Buin in July 1943. The many months of training now paid off for PO1/c Okano for he quickly blossomed in combat, scoring around a dozen victories in this theatre of operations. In November now CPO Okano was transferred to the 331st AG, with whom he participated in combats over western New Guinea, before returning to the mainland.

WO Okano ended the war attached to the 701st Squadron of the 343rd AG – the so-called 'Squadron of Experts'. He achieved 19 victories.

## Warrant Officer Sekizen Shibayama

Sekizen Shibayama was one of 'Rabaul's Last Eagles', a member of a guerrilla fighter squadron abandoned to its fate on New Britain.

Born in Saitama Prefecture in December 1923, he joined the navy and entered flight training in June 1940. After graduation in May 1942, Shibayama fulfilled the role of flight instructor at Yatabe airfield until posted to the 201st AG at Rabaul in September 1943 – he was subsequently transferred to the 253rd.

On 11 November Shibayama took off to intercept American carrier aircraft attacking Rabaul. As the novice pilot attempted to climb to altitude he experienced engine trouble, forcing him to unwittingly dive into a formation of eight Hellcats. In the resulting melee, future 10-kill ace Lt A B 'Chick' Smith of VF-9 clobbered Shibayama's Zero, sending it down in flames. The Japanese pilot glided his aircraft into Simpson Harbour and was later rescued – Smith claimed two A6Ms on this date.

Suffering from both a leg injury and malaria, Shibayama was grounded and saw no further action until the 253rd retreated to Truk Island where, as one of a handful of sick and injured pilots, he was left behind as the group continued its retreat northwards. A number of mechanics had also been abandoned on Truk, and they set about salvaging around a dozen Zero fighters from wrecks, thus creating a new squadron. Because of his combat experience, Shibayama and WO Shigeo Fukumoto were tasked with training half a dozen other pilots during the lull in fighting.

On 3 March 1944 seven Zeroes encountered F4Us of VMF-223 during a training flight over Tobera Airfield. In the short combat which ensued, the Japanese claimed five victories, including one to Shibayama (no F4Us were actually lost). Another scrap followed nine days later, this time involving F4Us from VMF-222. The Japanese claimed two, but again no Corsairs were lost – two Zeroes were, however, destroyed.

For the remainder of the war, Shibayama flew a number of patrol and bombing missions against American forces, and by August 1945 the unit was comprised of just two airworthy Zeroes. When Sekizen Shibayama was notified of the final surrender at at Kara (Buin) airfield, he was awaiting orders to make a solo suicide attack against approaching enemy warships. By his own reckoning he had attained 13 victories.

In August 1971 the veteran ace was reunited with his old Zero after it had been recovered from Simpson Harbour. The remarkable reunion took place in Bakersfield, California, and an examination of his seat revealed that a .50 cal 'slug' had missed his 'crown jewels' by inches. Today, Shibayama resides in Tokyo.

## Chief Petty Officer Takeo Okumura

During the Pacific War few fighter pilots became a 'double ace-in-a-day', Takeo Okumura being one of those in this elite band – his claim of ten places him in the same league as top US Navy ace Cdr David McCampbell, who set the American record of nine destroyed and two damaged.

This extraordinary JNAF ace was born in Fukui Prefecture in February 1920. He enlisted in the navy at Kure in June 1935, and opting for a career in aviation, he was selected for flight training in February 1938. Okumura graduated in September of the same year.

Arriving in China just in time to participate in the final aerial actions of the conflict, Okumura was good from the very start. On 7 October 1940 seven A6M2 Zeroes of the 14th AG escorted 27 G3M 'Nell' bombers sent to raid Kunming. Whilst in the vicinity of the target CAF I-15 biplanes fighters attempted to intercept the 'Nells' but the Zeroes made short work of them, downing 13 in a matter of minutes – Okumura was credited with destroying four of them in what had been his first engagement.

As this mission clearly proved, the new Zero was vastly superior to anything the Chinese could boast in their arsenal, and fighter opposition all but ceased following the A6M2's introduction in August 1940. Indeed, Okamura's quartet of kills on 7 October were the 20-year-old pilot's only victories of the China War. Returning to Japan, he subsequently helped train pilots until July 1942, when he was assigned to the carrier *Ryujo*.

It was in the Solomons that Okumura became a master of dogfighting. On 24 August, he was escorting torpedo-bombers sent to attack American ships at Guadalcanal when they were intercepted by into Wildcats led by legendary ace Capt Marion Carl of VMF-223. A turbulent dogfight ensued, and Okumura became separated from his flight, who reported him lost upon returning to *Ryujo*, although he later returned alive – Carl claimed four kills (out of an eventual tally of 18.5) during this action.

When Okumura's first tour of duty in the Solomons ended, he had achieved 14 recognised aerial victories. He returned to Japan in December, but was posted back to the frontline in July 1943 as a member of the 201st AG, flying from their base at Buin.

Okumura's ten-kill haul came on 14 September during a massive Allied attack on Buin. The Japanese sortied over 200 Zeroes from the 201st and the 204th AGs in opposition, and in three separate missions during the course of the day, Okumura accounted for an F4U, a B-24 (shared), two P-40s, five F6F Hellcats and an SBD. After the battle, Adm Jinichi

CPO Takeo Okumura became a double ace-in-a-day when he downed ten aircraft during three missions on 14 September 1943. He received a coveted ceremonial sword from VAdm Jinichi Kusaka for his actions (*Y Izawa*)

Kusaka, CO of the 11th Air Fleet at Rabaul, presented the ace with a ceremonial sword for distinguished service. Frustratingly for Okumura, individual credits were no longer being recorded due to a naval directive issued in June 1943, although his claim was unofficially touted as being the highest one-day score ever achieved by a JNAF pilot in action.

Eight days later Okumura failed to return from a bomber escort mission against a convoy sighted near Cape Cretin, New Guinea, the 35 Zeroes sortied being attacked by P-38s (432nd FS) and P-40s (35th FG).

CPO Takeo Okumura was subsequently recommended for a double rank promotion due to his distinguished record, but this was never realised. Four of his victories from the China War were officially recognised, and it is said he achieved roughly 50 victories in the Solomons.

## Warrant Officer Masaaki Shimakawa

Masaaki Shimakawa holds the distinction of being the top surviving JNAF ace of his native Tokushima Prefecture. Born in December 1921 as the youngest of five brothers, he joined the Sasebo Marines on 1 June 1939, thus realising his boyhood dream. This same dream quickly turned to harsh reality, however, for as a lowly enlisted man, Shimakawa was treated very poorly, being constantly hit. His contempt for officers grew.

Shimakawa decided to become an aviator, completing carrier fighter training in August 1940 and receiving an assignment to the Oita AG, followed in October 1941 by a posting the newly-formed Tainan AG.

On the opening day of the Pacific War, Shimakawa was the third wingman in the trio of Gitaro Miyazaki and Toshio Ota, both of whom went on to become distinguished aces. The Tainan and 3rd AGs combined to attack airfields in the Philippines, and during his baptism of fire, he claimed a P-35 over Del Carmen.

The Tainan AG then became involved in an 'air extermination' campaign over the Dutch East Indies, Shimakawa flying as wingman to Saburo Sakai. On 28 February 1942 he sortied with Sakai and witnessed his mentor shoot down a F2A Buffalo with miraculous skill, resolving at the same time to learn from this master. The young novice firmly believed that the export version of the Buffaloes (B-339Bs) were flown tenaciously by the Dutch, holding their own against the Zeroes of the Tainan AG.

When the group left for Rabaul in April 1942, Shimakawa was assigned to the 6th AG, boarding the carrier *Kaga*. During the Battle of Midway, he was thrown from the deck of his carrier into the sea as it sank, and while many of his comrades were sucked downed with the doomed vessel, he managed to survive – the 6th AG was virtually wiped out at Midway.

Reformed in Japan as part of the 204th AG, the survivors of the 6th were sent to the Solomons in August 1942. Flying from Bougainville, Shimakawa was involved in many fierce contests, as later recounted;

'The F4Fs at Guadalcanal were extremely tough fellows. We were confident in our skills and we were evenly matched. Our biggest enemies were long-range missions and bad weather. Many pilots lost their lives to stupid operational causes and not to enemy pilots.'

On 11 January 1943 Shimakawa and seven comrades attacked Wildcats of VMF-121 out of the sun over Guadalcanal, the Zero pilots overwhelming their counterparts in the F4Fs and forcing them into a

WO Nobuo Ogiya of the 204th AG was an expert marksman, and during one 18-day period he downed 13 enemy aircraft to set a naval record (*Y Izawa*)

PO Masaaki Shimakawa survived the sinking of his carrier *Kaga* during the battle of Midway. Having dodged enemy bullets and shot down eight fighters, he then fell victim to a malaria-carrying mosquito (*Maru*)

protective Lufbery circle. Upon seeing his comrades in trouble, Marine Gunner Ed Zielinski joined the circle in the opposite direction, scattering the Zeroes, and saving his comrades' lives.

During this radical manoeuvre Zielinski's F4F was damaged, and he now found himself alone, trying to nurse his crippled fighter back to base. After thoroughly scanning his instrument panel to check on his engine's vital signs, he glanced back out of his cockpit and was horrified to see a Zero flying on his wing! Its pilot made no attempt to attack the American, although the latter was rather unnerved by his opponent's stare. As the American contemplated ramming the Zero in order to bring the uneven contest to a swift end, the A6M suddenly dove down, looped in front of the Wildcat and repositioned itself on the Marine's tail – but did not fire. The Zero repeated this manoeuvre and the American pressed his gun button as the fighter looped in front of him. The guns remained silent, however, as the Zero completed its roll and was last seen heading for Munda. When asked about this incident many years later, Shimakawa responded, 'It could have been me, but I don't remember it quite like that'.

In a classic example of overclaiming, in the wake of this memorable encounter, the Zero pilots were credited with 18 victories for just one loss, whilst the Marines claimed ten kills and one probable for a single Wildcat shot down – Shimakawa added two victories to his tally.

While at Bougainville, Shimakawa was stricken down with a severe case of malaria and subsequently sent back to Japan aboard a hospital ship in March 1943. After his recovery, he became an instructor with the Omura AG and served with various units until war's end.

Masaaki Shimakawa downed eight aircraft and assisted, or shared, in the destruction of another 12-13. He passed away on 25 September 1997.

## Ensign Shigetoshi Kudo

Shigetoshi Kudo was a pioneer nightfighter pilot in the JNAF who helped formulate effective techniques to counter bombers in the South Pacific.

Born into a farming family in February 1920 in Oita Prefecture, he joined the navy in 1937. Kudo's path to becoming a premier fighter pilot was unspectacular, for his first role in the JNAF was as a mechanic. Switching to flying, he trained as a reconnaissance pilot and in October 1941 was assigned to the Tainan AG, with whom he duly saw combat in both the Philippines and Dutch East Indies.

During the early morning of 29 August 1942, B-17s from Port Moresby raided Rabaul, and somehow Kudo managed to get above the the formation in his C5M Type 98 'Babs' recce aircraft and claim a bomber destroyed and a second as a probable thanks to the use of an aerial burst bomb. These night raids were designed to rob the Japanese defenders of much-needed sleep, rather than to destroy important targets (bombing accuracy was minimal). Allied bomber crews considered such sorties as 'milk runs', because anti-aircraft fire was inaccurate and there were no nightfighters in-theatre.

Rabaul's first effective nocturnal fighter was the J1N1 Gekko ('Irving') fast twin-engined long-range recce aircraft. It was equipped with a pair of upward and downward firing 20 mm cannon, which were initially deemed as being ridiculous by staff officers at Naval GHQ and fiercely

Rabaul's 'King of the Night', PO1/c Shigetoshi Kudo, poses with a ceremonial sword and citation from VAdm Jinichi Kusaka in July 1943. His pioneering efforts against four-engined bombers over Rabaul helped the JNAF formulate night-fighting tactics that were later flown against B-29s over Japan (*K Osuo*)

CPO Yoshimi Hidaka of the 204th AG was also an escort pilots on the Adm Yamamoto mission. He claimed one P-38 probable during this sortie and was subsequently killed on 7 June 1943 over the Russells. He had claimed 20 victories by the time of his death (*Maru*)

The 253rd AG personnel pose for a group shot at Tobera Airfield, Rabaul, in February 1944. Three of the JNAF's top aces are sitting in the second row, namely Sadamu Komachi (second from right), Shigeo Fukumoto (third from right) and Tetsuzo Iwamoto (fourth from right). The unit began pulling out to Truk soon after this photo was taken, beginning 20 February 1944. Disabled pilots, along with 12 unserviceable A6Ms, were left behind, leaving Rabaul to its fate (*Y Izawa*)

resisted. Cdr Yasuna Kozono, deputy commander of the Tainan AG and instigator of the weapons fitment, persisted with the arrangement, however, and when the first Gekko arrived at Rabaul on 10 May 1943, CPO Shigetoshi Kudo was ordered to go and test it in combat.

Eleven days later, at 0320, Kudo scored the first Gekko nightfighter victory over Rabaul after he and observer Lt(jg) Akira Sugawara encountered B-17E 41-9244 of the 64th BS, flown by Maj Paul Williams, at 0320. Slipping beneath the Flying Fortress undetected, Kudo raked the undersides of the bomber with devastating effect. 'I heard one dull explosion, then a series of smaller ones. The ship wrenched to the left and shuddered . . .' sole survivor M/Sgt Gordon Manuel later recalled.

More was yet to come before daybreak, however, for Kudo and Sugawara found another B-17 at 0408, although they failed to get into an effective firing position. Twenty minutes later, he manoeuvred his aircraft beneath a second 64th BS B-17 (41-9011) and sent it down in flames. CPO Kudo had expended 178 rounds in destroying two B-17s. Cdr Kozono's 'wild scheme' had been fully validated.

During the course of June, CPO Kudo destroyed a total of five B-17s at night, with a sortie on 26 June resulting in a double victory – the sole survivor from either crew was 2Lt Jose Holguin from B-17 (41-2430) of the 65th BS, who parachuted into Japanese territory and was made a PoW.

Kudo's last recognised night kill occurred on 7 July 1943 when he downed a Hudson over Buin airfield. The following month the 23-year-old 'night hawk' was awarded a coveted ceremonial sword by Adm Junichi Kusaka, commander of the 11th Air Fleet at Rabaul, in recognition of his distinguished service.

Initially, the Americans believed that their night losses were due to operational reasons, although it wasn't long before they realised that JNAF nightfighters were the culprits. Consequently, the USAAF changed from night to daylight attacks, thus putting the Gekkos out of business. Following this tactical change Kudo returned to Japan in February 1944 and was assigned to the Yokosuka AG. He was severely

PO3/c Hiroshi Shibagaki (centre, third row from bottom) of the 204th AG claimed his first victory on 7 November 1943 at Rabaul. By the time he was killed on 22 January 1944, he had achieved 13 officially recognised aerial victories. Shibagaki was one of the few pilots in this post-Midway flight training class to become an ace (*Y Izawa*)

injured in a landing accident in May 1945 whilst still flying with this group, his wounds effectively ending his war career – in 1960, Kudo died from complications resulting from his old landing injury.

Ens Shigetoshi Kudo achieved nine recognised aerial victories, earning him the moniker of 'King of the Night' for his nocturnal prowess.

## Warrant Officer Hideo Watanabe

The Allied counter offensive in the Solomons began taking such a toll of Zero fighter units, and their irreplaceable commanders, that veteran enlisted men such as Hideo Watanabe were forced to step into positions of leadership – a role in which the young pilot performed admirably well.

Born into a farming family in Fukushima Prefecture in June 1920, Watanabe joined the navy at Yokosuka soon after turning 17 and completed his flight training in November 1941. As one of the last pilots trained prior to the outbreak of the pre-Pacific War, Watanabe was posted to the Marshalls-based Chitose AG in March 1942. About a year later he transferred to the 204th AG at Bougainville, seeing much action.

June 1943 proved to be a disastrous month for the 204th, for it lost a number of veteran flight leaders. On the 7th CPO Yoshimi Hidaka (20 victories) and PO1/c Yasuji Okazaki were both killed, whilst PO2/c Kenji

CPO Hideo Watanabe assumed a position of leadership within the 204th AG despite being an enlisted man. For his fighting spirit and distinguished service, he was awarded a ceremonial sword by VAdm Jinichi Kusaka

Veteran fighter pilot WO Shigeo Fukumoto led Rabaul's 'Guerrilla Air Force' of eight Zero fighters after the 253rd AG had retreated to Truk. Having survived the war with an impressive score of 72 victories, he was killed in a road accident in December 1945 (*K Osuo*)

Japan's Asahi Newspaper sent a reporter to Rabaul in January 1944 to interview pilots, but his articles were heavily exaggerated so as to minimise the tremendous losses being suffered by the JNAF. The pilots in this view are, from left to right, Takashi Kaneko, Masajiro Kawato, the reporter and Yoshinobu Ikeda (*Y Ikeda*)

Yanagiya was severely wounded – these three veterans had been a part of the escort for the ill-fated Adm Yamamoto mission. On 16 June another crippling blow was delivered when group leader, Lt Zenjiro Miyano, and Lt(jg) Takeshi Morizaki (squadron leader and Yamamoto mission escort pilot) failed to return. With a lack of qualified officer pilots and a shortage of warrant officers, CPO Watanabe assumed command of the squadron and flew as formation leader.

Watanabe plunged into the enemy formations with as much vigour as his predecessors had done, trying to lead his demoralised pilots through example. This tactic almost cost him his life, however. In the late afternoon of 26 August he single-handedly attacked a B-24 which had raided Buin, quickly shooting it down – he also claimed a Wildcat (none were involved in this combat). Escorting the Liberators on this day were F4U Corsairs from VMF-214 and -215, these aircraft engaging the Zeroes soon after Watanabe's audacious attack. The JNAF ace was hit hard by a Corsair that manoeuvred in behind him, a fragment from a .50 cal round striking him in the back of the head and exiting through his right eye.

In order to shake of his assailant, the wounded pilot violently threw his Zero into a dive, only pulling up at wave top height. Despite his injuries Watanabe somehow made it back to base and carried out a safe landing. While recovering in the hospital at Rabaul, Adm Junichi Kusaka, CO of the 11th Air Fleet, honoured the young aviator with a ceremonial sword for distinguished service. He duly returned to Japan by ship for further hospitalisation, and in June 1945 he was posted to the 1081st Transport Group.

Hideo Watanabe was officially credited with 16 victories. He now resides in Fukushima Prefecture.

## Warrant Officer Ryoji Ohara

Ryoji Ohara gained considerable combat experience in the Solomons fighting F4U Corsairs – and lived to tell the tale. Born in Miyagi Prefecture in February 1921, he joined the navy as soon as he was old enough, and subsequently graduated from flight training in July 1942.

Ohara was sent to the 6th AG base at Buin in October as a replacement pilot, recording his first victory on 23 October 1942 when his unit fought ten Wildcats of VMF-212 over Guadalcanal (no US aircraft were lost).

On 13 May 1943 Ohara was flying as wingman to air group leader Lt Zenjiro Miyano when a combined force of 54 Zeroes attacked Marine F4Us over the Russell Islands. Diving out of the sun from 24,000 ft, the JNAF pilots bounced the flight of five VMF-124 Corsairs, which were circling at 20,000 ft. Ohara managed to shoot down the Marine's leader, Maj William Gise, on his first pass before a wild dogfight ensued.

Upon disengaging from the battle, Ohara became separated from his flight, and was set upon by two Corsairs. One of his opponents was 1Lt William Cannon, who chased Ohara half way to New Georgia Island, before the Japanese pilot chose to fight for his survival. On a desperate counterattacking manoeuvre, Ohara fired on his pursuers and claimed one destroyed – Cannon's Corsair was holed three times by 20 mm rounds but still made it home. Having seen off his attackers, Ohara was forced to make an emergency landing at Kolombangara Island, where he counted 38 bullet holes in his Zero.

Ohara fought with distinction with the 204th AG before returning to Japan and joining the Yokosuka AG. He subsequently flew home defence missions until 17 August 1945, his last sortie seeing him engage photo-recce B-32 Dominators over Tokyo.

Dubbed the 'Killer of Rabaul', WO Ryoji Ohara claimed 48 kills. After the war he joined the Japanese Self-Defence Air Force, before running a simulator school for airline pilots. Now fully retired, he lives in Tokyo.

## Lieutenant Zenjiro Miyano

Zenjiro Miyano was the great leader of the 204th AG whose innovative ideas – he was the first JNAF pilot to adopt the effective 'fighter four' formation – and leadership skills remain revered to this day.

He was born in Osaka and entered the Navy Academy with the 65th Class, graduating from flight training in April 1940.

As a member of the 12th AG, Miyano was posted to the China War, but arrived too late to see combat. He subsequently became a division officer in the 3rd AG and participated in the raid on Luzon on the first day of the Pacific War. During this sortie he claimed his first aerial victory.

When the 3rd AG moved into the Dutch East Indies, Miyano continued to fly combat air patrols. On 3 March 1942 he led his Zeroes on a long-range attack against the Western Australian port town of Broome, destroying 22 aircraft (predominantly flying boats full of Dutch evacuees) and numerous installations and vehicles.

While returning to base with his two wingmen, Miyano encountered a Dutch DC-3 flown by Capt Ivan Smirnoff, Russia's second highest scoring ace (with 12 victories) of World War 1. The Dakota was packed with military personnel, and their families, fleeing Bandung, on Java, for the safety of Australia. The three Zeroes fired repeatedly at the transport, and although Smirnoff was wounded in the attack, he still managed to crash land the damaged aircraft on a beach. Prior to take-off, Smirnoff had been entrusted with a small sealed box containing a fortune in jewels, and this was accidentally lost in the water during the evacuation of the aircraft. Some of its contents was later recovered over the next few years.

The following month the 6th AG was organised, with Lt Miyano as its division officer. Embarked on the carrier *Junyo*, Miyano and his men headed for the Aleutians, with plans to assault Midway after the completion of their initial task. On 3 June Miyano led a six-Zero escort for 'Val' dive-bombers as part of a multi-carrier attack force sent to strike at Dutch Harbor. The following day at around 1800 hours, Miyano led his Zeroes back to the target, although this time P-40Es from the USAAF 11th FS opposed the strike. The Japanese were credited with six Warhawks destroyed while the Americans claimed a Zero and three 'Vals'. The *Junyo*

WO Ryoji Ohara was known to his comrades as the 'Killer of Rabaul'. He held his own against the dreaded F4U Corsairs in wild dogfights across the Solomons, one of his early victims being Maj William Gise, CO of VMF-124 (*Maru*)

Lt Zenjiro Miyano was the first JNAF pilot to adopt the effective four-fighter flight formation used by the Americans. Under his leadership, his unit claimed over 200 victories (*Maru*)

failed to participate in the Battle of Midway, surviving the disaster to return to port on 24 June.

Due to the fierce counterattack by Allied forces in the Solomons, an immediate need for both fighters and pilots was conveyed to the Naval High Command, and on 7 October 1942 Lt Miyano led 27 Zeroes (along with equipment and ground personnel) aboard the carrier *Zuiho*, bound for Rabaul. Once fully assembled on land, the unit moved to their forward base at Buin, where the 6th AG was reorganised into the 204th AG.

Once in the frontline, Lt Miyano immediately set about analysing American fighter tactics and devising his own countering manoeuvres, which included copying the USAAC's successful four-aircraft flight formation and developing new fighter-bombing tactics. In March 1943 Miyano became group leader, and while most officers were inexperienced and relied on enlisted men to insure their survival, he was always in the lead, setting an example to others (claiming many kills in the process).

On 16 June 1943 Miyano's luck ran out, for he was shot down and killed while escorting dive-bombers sent to attack enemy positions at Lunga. His score stood at 16 at the time of his death.

The Naval All Units Proclamation No 72, issued in conjunction with a posthumous double promotion to the rank of commander, stated that Lt Miyano's unit had destroyed 228 aircraft in the air and damaged 76.

## Lieutenant Chitoshi Isozaki

Chitoshi Isozaki was one of the 'grand old men' of the navy's fighter force, having seen frontline service for over 13 years. Widely respected throughout the ranks, he had the rare distinction of attaining officer status from his humble beginnings as a seaman recruit.

Isozaki was born on 12 January 1913 in Aichi Prefecture, and after graduation from middle school, he joined the navy. Entered flight training in October 1932, he graduated in March of the following year and then served as a flight instructor. One of his pupils during this tuitional phase in his career was the renowned ace Saburo Sakai.

When the China War erupted in 1937, Isozaki flew combat missions from the carrier *Ryujo* and *Kaga*. At the end of 1939, he was posted to the 12th AG and engaged in further combats, but scored no victories.

In October 1941, now WO Isozaki was transferred to the Tainan AG and served in the Dutch East Indies, before returning to Japan to serve as an instructor once more at Omura airfield when his former unit was posted to Rabaul.

In April 1943 Isozaki was promoted to the rank of ensign after more than ten years of service. It was rare for enlisted men to reach officer status, and Isozaki's promotion was a testament to his skill and leadership. In the same month, he was ordered to join the 251st AG at Rabaul.

On 16 June 1943 Ens Isozaki recorded his first kill when he fought US and New Zealand fighters over the Russells. By the time he was sent home to Japan in March 1944, he had served with both the 204th and 201st AGs at Bougainville and Rabaul, and achieved close to a dozen victories.

In Japan, Isozaki served briefly with the 302nd AG at Atsugi alongside fellow old timer Ens Sadaaki Akamatsu – they both trained pilots hard, and several veterans credit their survival to these two 'old masters'.

Although Lt Chitoshi Isozaki saw service during the China War, he failed to score his first victory until June 1943. Despite being overwhelmed by the Americans, Isozaki was still able to achieve more than a dozen victories by war's end (*Y Izawa*)

In May 1945 Lt(jg) Isozaki joined the elite 343rd AG, which was equipped exclusively with the Shiden-Kai ('George') fighter. As a division officer in the 301st Squadron, he saw very little combat in the remaining months of the war.

Chitoshi Isozaki logged more than 4000 flight hours during his career. This modest gentleman stated that he never knew exactly what his tally was, but 12+ victories seems to be accurate. As a respected senior member of the 343rd AG and Zero Fighter Pilots Association, he ran a small noodle shop in Matsuyama City until he passed away on 20 June 1993.

**This early model A6M2 was abandoned by the Tainan AG at Rabaul in late 1942 after suffering battle damage (*via Aerospace Publishing*)**

**A single A6M2 (in the foreground) and a quartet of A6M5s (in the background) are seen running up at Buin (Kahili airstrip) in late 1943. These aircraft are 582nd AG (ex-*Zuikaku* AG) aircraft (*via Robert C Mikesh*)**

# CENTRAL PACIFIC TO THE PHILIPPINES

B y mid 1944 the fate of Japan's war effort was sealed as the American naval 'juggernaut' bypassed various enemy strongholds in the South Pacific in their race toward the Philippines. Allied submarines prowled the sea lanes while aircraft bombed and strafed airfields, shipping and supply depots.

As the Allied forces pounded Rabaul, Adm Chester Nimitz led his fleet through the Central Pacific. The pattern adopted by the Americans would see heavy naval bombardment firstly soften up Japanese defences, before Marines, followed by army infantry, stormed the islands. Using such tactics, the Gilbert Islands were under Allied control by the end of November 1943. In the immediate aftermath of invasion, US Navy engineers immediately created airstrips in the Gilberts to enable aircraft to attack the Marshall Islands. The latter subsequently proved difficult for the Japanese to defend, as hundreds of small coral atolls were scattered over 400,000 square miles.

**Pilots prepare to climb into their fuelled and armed up A6M5cs somewhere in the Philippines in 1944 (*via Aerospace Publishing*)**

**With his Sakae 21 throbbing away in front of him, and his silk scarf ballooning out around his neck as the slipstream builds up with the increased acceleration of the fighter, an anonymous A6M5 pilot takes off to do battle with superior Allied forces perhaps for the last time (*via Aerospace Publishing*)**

The 252nd AG had been providing a modicum of air defence for the Marshalls from their bases on Roi and Wake Islands since February 1943, although they had seen very little action until September when B-24s began to raid their airfields. On 5 October 1943, US carrier aircraft attacked Wake Island, with Hellcats from the carriers *Cowpens, Essex, Lexington* and *Yorktown* overwhelming the 26 Zeroes sent up to oppose the strike – 16 A6Ms failed to return.

When the alarm sounded at Roi, Lt Yuzo Tsukamoto mustered six Zeroes as escorts for seven 'Betty' bombers sent to bolster Wake's defences. Rather than help defend the island, the formation simply became more Hellcat 'fodder' as it was intercepted by navy fighters some 30 miles short of their destination. Only three aircraft, including Tsukamoto's, eventually landed on Wake.

With few aircraft remaining, the 252nd AG tried to counterattack, but were detected by Allied radar and intercepted every time. Although about 30 Zeroes remained on Taroa by December, carrier air raids on the island destroyed most of the fighters on the ground, while the rest were shot down in one-sided dogfights. Their last combat occurred on 29 January, and like most of the preceding engagements, achieved nothing.

The path was now wide open for an assault on the Marianas Islands. Should they fall, Allied forces would then be centrally placed for a direct attack on Japan, the Philippines and New Guinea. JNAF land- and carrier-based aircraft assembled to defend against the anticipated onslaught, and on 11 June 1944 the bombardment of Guam commenced.

On 19 June, Adm Marc Mischer's US Task Force 58 – composed of 18 carriers and over 475 Hellcats – engaged VAdm Jisaburo Ozawa's carrier armada of nine carriers and over 450 aircraft. The Battle of the Philippine Sea was the last time the Imperial Navy possessed enough strength to challenge the US Pacific Fleet. Although strong in numbers, JNAF squadrons were hampered by a lack of co-ordinated battle tactics and well-trained pilots. The end result was the total overwhelming of Japanese formations by swarms of marauding Hellcats, who cut them to ribbons – the aerial massacre was so one-sided that it was dubbed the 'Marianas Turkey Shoot' by participating F6F pilots. The 343rd AG was literally destroyed in this action, being forced to disband on 10 July.

When the smoke had finally cleared from the two-day battle, the Japanese had lost the carriers *Shokaku, Taiho* and *Hiyo*, and suffered crippling damage to the *Zuikaku* and *Chiyoda*. Also lost were over 300 aircraft and veteran pilots and aircrews. This was Japan's worst military disaster to date, and it effectively 'broke the back' of the JNAF in the Pacific.

RAdm Joseph Clark, commanding TF58.1, now headed for another show down at Iwo Jima.

This underside view of an A6M5 Zeke 52 reveals the staple JNAF fighter in near-perfect planform. The Model 52 was the most prolific of all Zero variants, with over 6000 being built (*via Aerospace Publishing*)

His pilots had scored heavily on 15 June over the island, and they now wanted an encore – the 'Marianas Turkey Shoot' had simply whetted their voracious appetite. Although Iwo Jima was just a tiny volcanic island, its strategic position made it a highly-valued prize, for Zero fighters based there posed a serious threat to B-29s sent to bomb Japan.

The Yokosuka AG was ordered to Iwo Jima in June, arriving during a lull in the bombardment. On the 24th, in their first combat over the island, pilots from the unit – as well as members of the 252nd and 301st AGs – were badly mauled by TF58.1 Hellcats. Over 80 Zeroes had sortied, and only around half had returned.

The second and third combats for Iwo Jima's Zeroes occurred on 3-4 July when, despite heroic efforts by the defenders, the Yokosuka AG lost 22 veteran pilots, including their leader, Lt Sadao Yamaguchi (an accomplished ace with 12 victories). American warships later destroyed many aircraft on the airfields with their 'big guns', leaving the distinguished Yokosuka AG to become a unit without aircraft. The survivors were evacuated back to the mainland, and the island was abandoned to its fate.

As the US Task Force swept through the Central Pacific, the Japanese prepared for the onslaught by ordering the 1st Air Fleet at Davao, in the Philippines, to stop the Allied advance. This was an impossible task, however, for the fleet's units lacked trained pilots, fuel and aircraft. The VAdm Ozawa's humiliating defeat at the Battle of the Philippine Sea forced the JNAF to adopt desperate measures in their fight with the Allies.

The invasion of the Philippines commenced on 23 October 1944 with troop landings on Leyte. The subsequent naval clash, christened the Battle of Leyte Gulf, saw the demise of Japan's two greatest battleships, the *Yamato* and *Musashi*.

With events going from bad to worse for the Japanese, VAdm Takijiro Onishi – CO of the 1st Air Fleet – gave birth to the dreaded *Kamikaze* Suicide Corps, his radical idea being to equip a Zero fighter with a 250-kg bomb and have volunteers crash themselves into the decks of aircraft carriers. The few remaining 'fighter' Zeroes were to act as escorts to protect the *kamikazes* from prowling enemy aircraft, plus record their results.

'We had no criticism about the *kamikaze* operations because we thought we had to die inevitably', recalled former Zero pilot Masahiro Mitsuda. 'We thought nothing of whether it would be a futile effort or not'.

Even officer pilots like Lt Cdr Iyozoh Fujita (hero at Midway) echoed these sentiments; 'We had few planes and no fuel to train pilots, so we had no other choice'.

With no hope of survival, pilots volunteered in droves for a chance to strike back at the enemy in a wave of hyper patriotism. As a further incentive, those *kamikaze* who died were promised double rank promotions.

The first successful suicide attack occurred on 25 October when bomb-laden Zeroes from the 201st AG sank the escort carrier *St Lo* and damaged six others. The news of this initial success spread like wildfire, renewing the sagging morale of an entire nation.

Allied forces were quick to enact countermeasures, however, with combat air patrols and destroyer pickets serving to insulate the carriers in their first line of defence. Further success therefore became more and more elusive as hundreds sortied into oblivion – the 201st AG wrote their obitu-

Ens Isamu Miyazaki was a chivalrous pilot who spared the life of an opponent flying a badly damaged Hellcat. His unit was destroyed in the Marshall Islands, although he survived, ending the war with 13 victories (*I Miyazaki*)

ary in the Philippines campaign.

Whilst Allied land forces invaded Luzon and became bogged down in ground action, the naval units continued their advance toward Japan.

## Ensign Isamu Miyazaki

Isamu Miyazaki once spared the life of an US fighter pilot, which was a chivalrous act totally foreign to the JNAF's philosophy of giving no quarter to the enemy.

Born in Kagawa Prefecture in October 1919, he enlisted in the navy in 1936 and served as a common sailor, before volunteering for fighter training. He completed the course in November 1941, and 12 months later he advanced to Rabaul with the 252nd AG

Ens Saburo Saito scored his first victory on 1 February 1943 – an F4F over Guadalcanal. Later fighting over Rabaul and Bougainville, he destroyed eight enemy aircraft during a one-week period. Saito claimed his final kill on 24 October 1944 east of Luzon, although he was seriously wounded during the same action when he force-landed on the shore of Lamon Bay. Repatriated to Japan, he ended the war with at least 18 victories (*Maru*)

Veteran pilots of the famous Yokosuka AG fought an overwhelming number of Hellcats over Iwo Jima during June and July 1944. The aces seen are; Ryoji Ohara (48 victories, front row, left), Masami Shiga (16 victories, back row, 2nd from left), Tomita Atake (10 victories, 3rd from left), and Kiyoshi Sekiya (11 victories, right) (*Y Izawa*)

Mabalacat Airfield, in the Philippines, is seen on 25 October 1944 as Lt Yukio Seki's *kamikaze* flight, with accompanying escorts, prepares to sortie in the first successful suicide attack carried out against US warships (*Maru*)

The caption for this official US Navy photograph reads, 'A Japanese *kamikaze* pilot taxiing his bomb-laden "Zero" fighter to take-off position on a Philippine airfield during the Leyte operations in October-November 1944. His comrades cheer as the plane passes between them' (*via Aerospace Publishing*)

On 12 November Miyazaki was of 30 Zeroes escort 19 torpedo-equipped 'Betty' bombers sent to attack American transports off Lunga Point. Marine pilots of VMF-112 and -121, together with USAAF P-400s, intercepted the Japanese formation and a great dogfight ensued – Miyazaki's first action ended with the destruction of an F4F.

The 252nd AG flew sorties from Rabaul, Ballale (Bougainville), Lae and Munda, during which time Miyazaki gained considerable experience through hard fought battles over the Solomons.

On 1 February 1943 the 252nd was ordered to the Marshall Islands, where the level of combat lessened until the autumn, when American carrier fighters attacked the Gilbert Islands. Miyazaki subsequently fought B-24s which had come to soften up targets for the impending invasion.

On 30 January 1944 Miyazaki fought in his air group's last battle. In his

The great ace WO Hiroyoshi Nishizawa became a reluctant instructor in the mass training of Zero pilots, and he is shown here in 1944 with his trainees. Back in the frontline, he provided the escort on 25 October 1944 for Lt Yukio Seki's *kamikazes*. The following day Nishizawa was shot down and killed in a transport aircraft (*Sakaida*)

Ens Yoshinao Kodaira commenced his combat career in China, and later fought in the Battles of the Coral Sea and the eastern Solomons, and over Guadalcanal. During the Battle of Leyte Gulf he shot down a Hellcat, but on 8 November he was injured in a take-off accident and sent back to Japan. He ended the war with 11 victories (*Sakaida*)

WO Kazuo Sugino first entered combat on 2 November 1943 over Rabaul when he shot down two aircraft He later joined the 634th AG and saw considerable action over Formosa and the Philippines, before ending the war as an instructor for *kamikaze* pilots. In over 495 missions he claimed 32 victories (*Maru*)

A veteran of Rabaul, CPO Takeo Tanimizu (see next chapter for his biography) subsequently served in Formosa with the Tainan AG during the summer and winter of 1944, battling with USAAF B-24s and P-51s. On 3 November 1944 he was shot down by a P-51 over Amoy Harbour, China, and survived with critical burns. Upon his recovery he volunteered for the *kamikaze*s but was rejected (*T Tanimizu*)

This rare photograph shows a training camera attached to the top wing of a veteran A6M2 Zero 21 – this modification was used strictly for tuitional purposes only. Lt Masatake Hayasaki (right) was an instructor pilot in the 256th AG at Lunghwa Airfield, Shanghai, China (*Hayasaki Family*)

Lt Ayao Shirane was a respected fighter-leader whose unit introduced the new 'George' fighter into combat against the Americans over the Philippines (*Y Izawa*)

second sortie four Zeroes fought an uneven dogfight which saw three of them sustain damage, forcing them to withdraw. Now alone, Miyazaki chanced upon a solitary damaged Hellcat flying 30 metres above the sea, and he tailed the American until satisfied that his opponent could not fight. Flying alongside, he stared at the pilot, who 'had such a pitiful expression on his face', the ace later recalled, that "I didn't have the heart to shoot him down, so I let him go'. Ens Fletcher Jones of VF-10 eventually ditched his fighter, but was drowned.

With the destruction of the 252nd AG, Miyazaki returned to Japan in February as one of only three surviving pilots. In January 1945 he joined the elite 343rd AG, flying home defence sorties until the surrender.

Isamu Miyazaki achieved at least 13 victories.

## Lieutenant Commander Ayao Shirane

When asked who were the greatest fighter-leaders of the JNAF, Ayao Shirane's name is always mentioned, along with Mochifumi Nango and several others. Shirane was born into a prominent family in Tokyo (1916), his father later becoming a cabinet secretary in the Japanese government. He graduated from the Naval Academy at Etajima in the 64th Class.

As a 'deck officer' graduate of the academy, Ens Shirane was given flight training and completed his course in March 1939, becoming a fighter pilot. Posted to the 12th AG in China, he participated in the raid on Chungking on 19 August 1940 when the new Zero fighter made its combat debut – Lt Tamotso Yokoyama led a dozen Zeroes on a bomber escort mission, although no enemy fighters were encountered.

On 13 September Lt(jg) Shirane led the 2nd division (six fighters) of 13 Zeroes, commanded by Lt Saburo Shindo, in the Zero fighter's true baptism of fire. After escorting 'Nell' bombers to Hankow, Chinese fighters rose to challenge the Japanese, and in the ensuing one-sided dogfight, the 13 JNAF fighter pilots claimed the destruction of all 27 enemy fighters. Shirane himself accounted for one aircraft destroyed – his first aerial victory. Adm Shigetaro Shimada, CO of the China Area Fleet, later issued a special unit commendation to mark this historic event.

When the Pacific War broke out, Lt Shirane was serving on the carrier *Akagi* as a division officer. Although he did not fly on the Pearl Harbor raid, he did participate in the Battle of Midway in June 1942, when he led 18 'Val' dive-bombers and nine Zero escorts in an attack on Midway Island itself. Upon completion of their task, the Shirane group returned to their carrier to perform combat air patrols over their ship, although they could not prevent the *Akagi* from being attacked by US dive-bombers – the vessel sank that night.

Lt Shirane was then transferred to the carrier *Zuikaku* to assume duties as their division officer. He stayed on in this position, seeing action in the Battle of the Eastern Solomons and the Battle of Santa Cruz, until November 1942, when he was posted to the land-based Yokosuka AG.

In November 1943 Shirane was assigned to the newly-organised 341st AG, this unit having originally be formed to make use of the new Shiden ('George') fighter. However, deliveries were seriously delayed, and it wasn't until February 1944 that the first handful of aircraft arrived just in time for training exercises to commence. In July the air group was split into two squadrons, and Shirane became CO of the 401st. Despite intensive training, the unit experienced numerous setbacks due to the inexperience of its pilots and design defects which plagued the new fighter.

In October Lt Cdr Shirane took his unit to Mabalacat airfield, on Luzon, where they saw immediate action. Attacking enemy forces at Leyte , they suffered heavy casualties at the hands of numerically-superior USAAF fighter groups.

On 24 November 1944 Ayao Shirane was killed in aerial combat with P-38s from the 433rd FS near Ponson Island, on the western coast of Leyte Island. At the time of his death he had nine officially recognised aerial victories to his credit.

Lt Cdr Shirane's superb organisational skills, and his ability to lead the rank and file, endeared him to both his subordinates and superiors.

## Ensign Minoru Honda

This young pilot had a miraculous career that even included returning from the 'dead'! Honda credited his wartime survival to the following three rules: 1) don't be over anxious for a kill; 2) know how and when to escape; and 3) keep nervous, be alert and spot the enemy first.

Minoru Honda was born in Kumamoto Prefecture in 1923, enlisting in the navy and entering flight training in October 1939. Whilst still under instruction he nearly killed himself when his aircraft became entangled with a target tow. He had vowed to hit his target at whatever cost due

Ens Minoru Honda suffered a great indignity at the hands of his superiors when he returned alive from a mission after being declared killed. He harboured a passionate hatred for the officer class, and also voiced his opposition to the *kamikaze* suicide attacks (*Y Izawa*)

to his prior inferior performance, and luckily for him, the target fell away at the last moment and his life was spared, although he subsequently received a severe reprimand from his superiors.

In April 1942 Honda was assigned to the Kanoya AG, his first combat occurring when he and his flight of eight intercepted nine RAF Buffaloes over Singapore. In his excitement at seeing the enemy, he failed to release his drop tank or fire his guns! In one of the worst displays of aerial combat discipline, Honda remembers, 'we all broke off individually and climbed and dove like wildmen. There wasn't a single kill on either side, and everyone escaped unharmed'. The 19-year-old neophyte with 95 hours of flight time in the Zero duly became separated from the rest during the aerial melee, and was the last to return to base. Another severe reprimand followed.

In September Honda advanced to Rabaul, where he fought in many aerial engagements over eastern New Guinea and the Solomons. During this period he was forced to make an emergency landing on Kolombangara Island, and when approached by a group of curious natives, Honda held up a bag of candy in one hand and a Browning automatic in the other. The natives were friendly, and tended to his needs for ten days until he was rescued.

In the meantime, PO1/c Honda had been written off for dead. For distinguished service, he had been given a rare posthumous double promotion, and expecting a hero's welcome on his return, he was once again chastised! His immediate superiors did not want to make a corrections in the casualty report for a lowly enlisted man, so for seven days straight, Honda was ordered to fly long-range combat missions alone into enemy territory in the hope that he would not return alive. Finally, when a senior officer learned of this matter, he was taken off the suicide missions, brought back to 'life', and stripped of his double promotion – such an increase in rank for a living enlisted man would have been unprecedented.

In April 1944 Honda was transferred to Fighter Squadron 407, and later fought in the Philippines. Here, he trained young novices for *kamikaze* attacks, which was a task that left him totally demoralised. Honda bitterly complained to his superiors about the stupidity of using his subordinates as human bombs.

His last assignment was with the elite 343rd AG flying home defence sorties against B-29s attacking southern Japan. Although a strict and unforgiving leader according to his surviving comrades, Honda owed his life to his tough training.

'One of our big problems was that we were educated that mind over might could win a war', Honda stated after the war. 'We fought by spirit while we were told that the Americans were lazy so-and-so's. This was not true. American pilots were very brave and extremely courageous. Yet unlike us, they would not take stupid chances. Our leadership wasn't as flexible as our enemy's. The Americans learned from their mistakes and developed better planes and battle techniques, while we clung religiously to the one-man Zero fighter "lone wolf" approach . . . what a mistake!'

Honda downed at least 17 enemy aircraft, although he estimates that he hit between 40 and 50 before he stopped counting. After the war, he became a test pilot and spent a lot of time in the USA flying the Mitsubishi MU-2.

# COLOUR PLATES

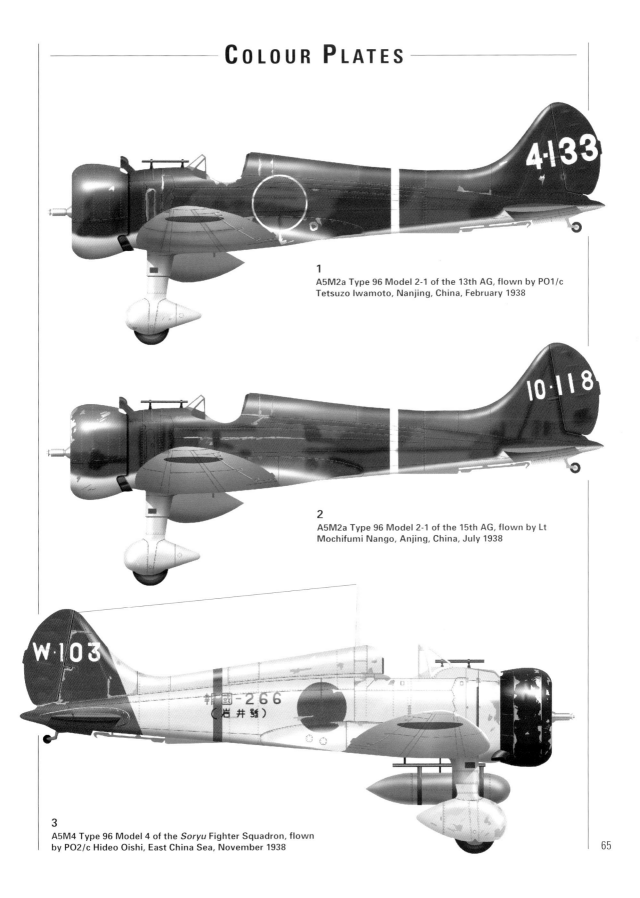

**1**
A5M2a Type 96 Model 2-1 of the 13th AG, flown by PO1/c
Tetsuzo Iwamoto, Nanjing, China, February 1938

**2**
A5M2a Type 96 Model 2-1 of the 15th AG, flown by Lt
Mochifumi Nango, Anjing, China, July 1938

**3**
A5M4 Type 96 Model 4 of the *Soryu* Fighter Squadron, flown
by PO2/c Hideo Oishi, East China Sea, November 1938

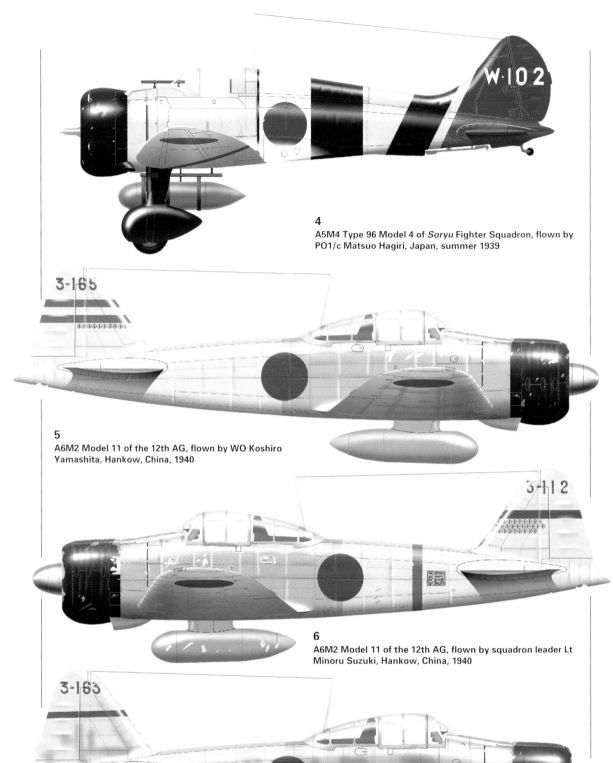

**4**
A5M4 Type 96 Model 4 of *Soryu* Fighter Squadron, flown by
PO1/c Matsuo Hagiri, Japan, summer 1939

**5**
A6M2 Model 11 of the 12th AG, flown by WO Koshiro
Yamashita, Hankow, China, 1940

**6**
A6M2 Model 11 of the 12th AG, flown by squadron leader Lt
Minoru Suzuki, Hankow, China, 1940

**7**
A6M2 Model 11 of the 12th AG, flown by PO2/c Tsutomu
Iwai, Hankow, China, 13 September 1940

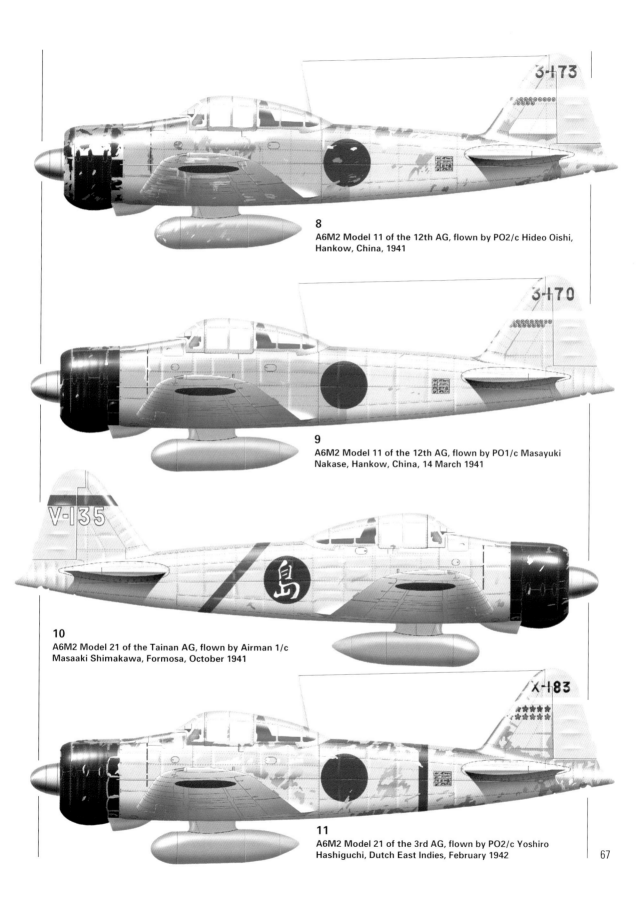

**8**
A6M2 Model 11 of the 12th AG, flown by PO2/c Hideo Oishi,
Hankow, China, 1941

**9**
A6M2 Model 11 of the 12th AG, flown by PO1/c Masayuki
Nakase, Hankow, China, 14 March 1941

**10**
A6M2 Model 21 of the Tainan AG, flown by Airman 1/c
Masaaki Shimakawa, Formosa, October 1941

**11**
A6M2 Model 21 of the 3rd AG, flown by PO2/c Yoshiro
Hashiguchi, Dutch East Indies, February 1942

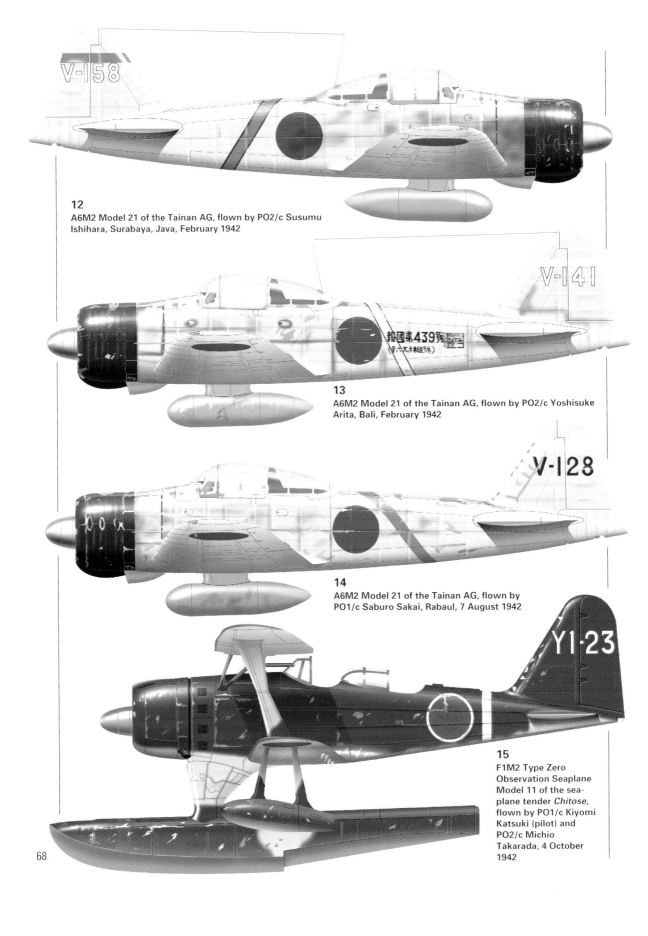

**12**
A6M2 Model 21 of the Tainan AG, flown by PO2/c Susumu Ishihara, Surabaya, Java, February 1942

**13**
A6M2 Model 21 of the Tainan AG, flown by PO2/c Yoshisuke Arita, Bali, February 1942

**14**
A6M2 Model 21 of the Tainan AG, flown by PO1/c Saburo Sakai, Rabaul, 7 August 1942

**15**
F1M2 Type Zero Observation Seaplane Model 11 of the seaplane tender *Chitose*, flown by PO1/c Kiyomi Katsuki (pilot) and PO2/c Michio Takarada, 4 October 1942

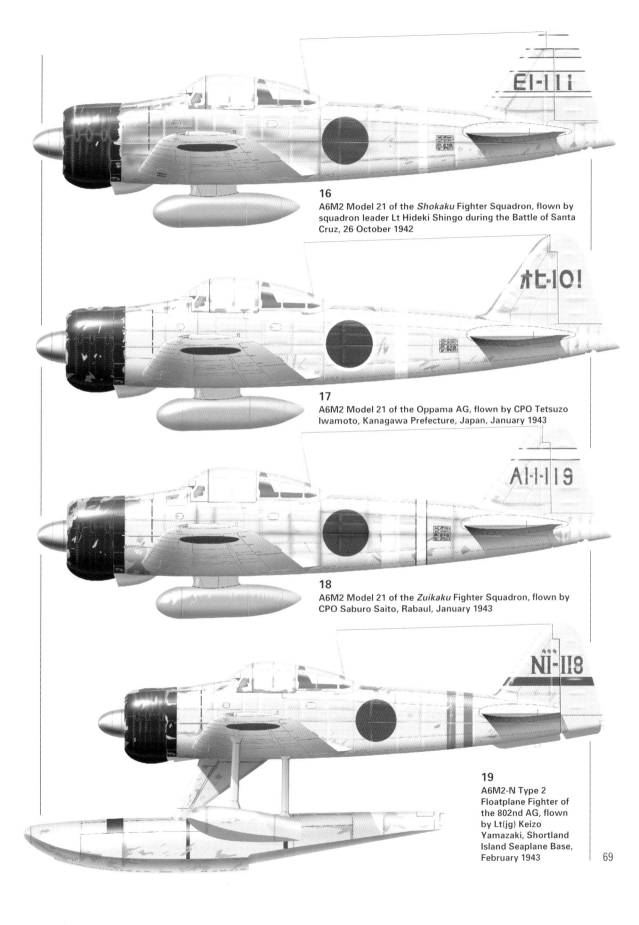

**16**
A6M2 Model 21 of the *Shokaku* Fighter Squadron, flown by
squadron leader Lt Hideki Shingo during the Battle of Santa
Cruz, 26 October 1942

**17**
A6M2 Model 21 of the Oppama AG, flown by CPO Tetsuzo
Iwamoto, Kanagawa Prefecture, Japan, January 1943

**18**
A6M2 Model 21 of the *Zuikaku* Fighter Squadron, flown by
CPO Saburo Saito, Rabaul, January 1943

**19**
A6M2-N Type 2
Floatplane Fighter of
the 802nd AG, flown
by Lt(jg) Keizo
Yamazaki, Shortland
Island Seaplane Base,
February 1943

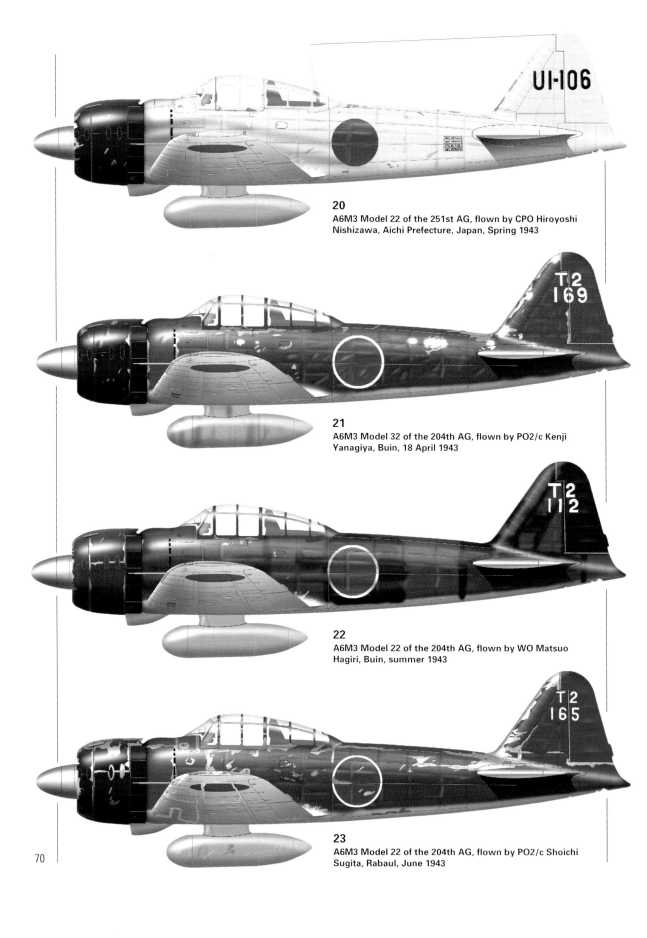

**20**
A6M3 Model 22 of the 251st AG, flown by CPO Hiroyoshi Nishizawa, Aichi Prefecture, Japan, Spring 1943

**21**
A6M3 Model 32 of the 204th AG, flown by PO2/c Kenji Yanagiya, Buin, 18 April 1943

**22**
A6M3 Model 22 of the 204th AG, flown by WO Matsuo Hagiri, Buin, summer 1943

**23**
A6M3 Model 22 of the 204th AG, flown by PO2/c Shoichi Sugita, Rabaul, June 1943

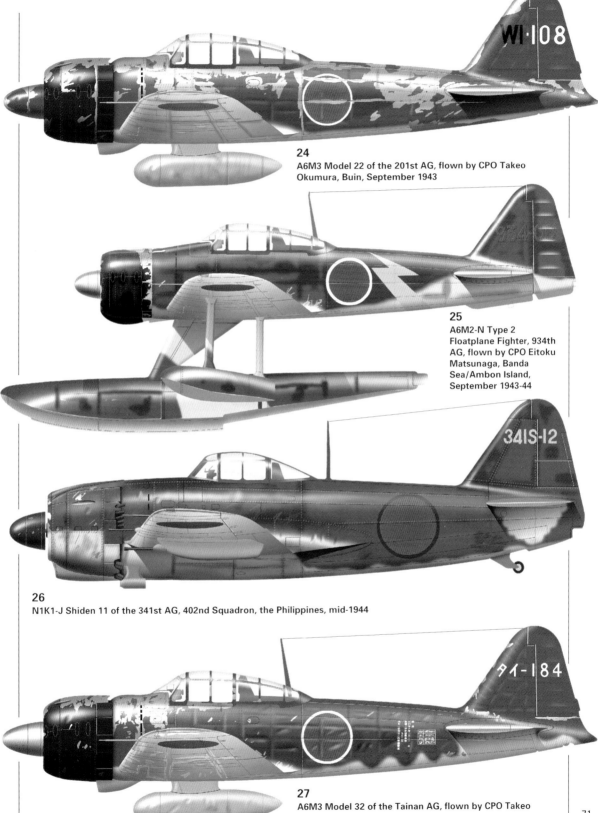

24
A6M3 Model 22 of the 201st AG, flown by CPO Takeo
Okumura, Buin, September 1943

25
A6M2-N Type 2
Floatplane Fighter, 934th
AG, flown by CPO Eitoku
Matsunaga, Banda
Sea/Ambon Island,
September 1943-44

26
N1K1-J Shiden 11 of the 341st AG, 402nd Squadron, the Philippines, mid-1944

27
A6M3 Model 32 of the Tainan AG, flown by CPO Takeo
Tanimizu, Tainan, Formosa, September 1944

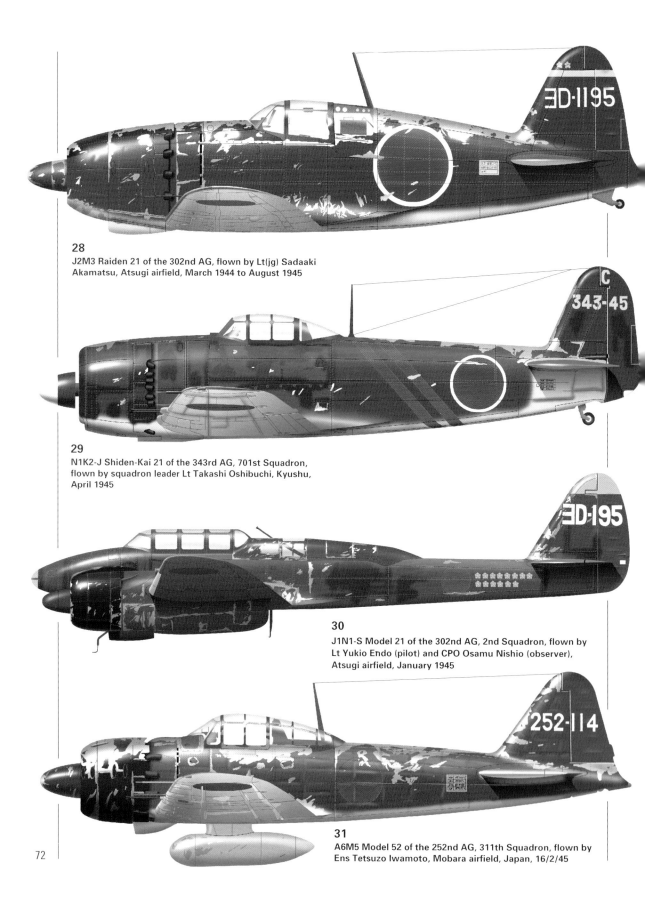

**28**
J2M3 Raiden 21 of the 302nd AG, flown by Lt(jg) Sadaaki
Akamatsu, Atsugi airfield, March 1944 to August 1945

**29**
N1K2-J Shiden-Kai 21 of the 343rd AG, 701st Squadron,
flown by squadron leader Lt Takashi Oshibuchi, Kyushu,
April 1945

**30**
J1N1-S Model 21 of the 302nd AG, 2nd Squadron, flown by
Lt Yukio Endo (pilot) and CPO Osamu Nishio (observer),
Atsugi airfield, January 1945

**31**
A6M5 Model 52 of the 252nd AG, 311th Squadron, flown by
Ens Tetsuzo Iwamoto, Mobara airfield, Japan, 16/2/45

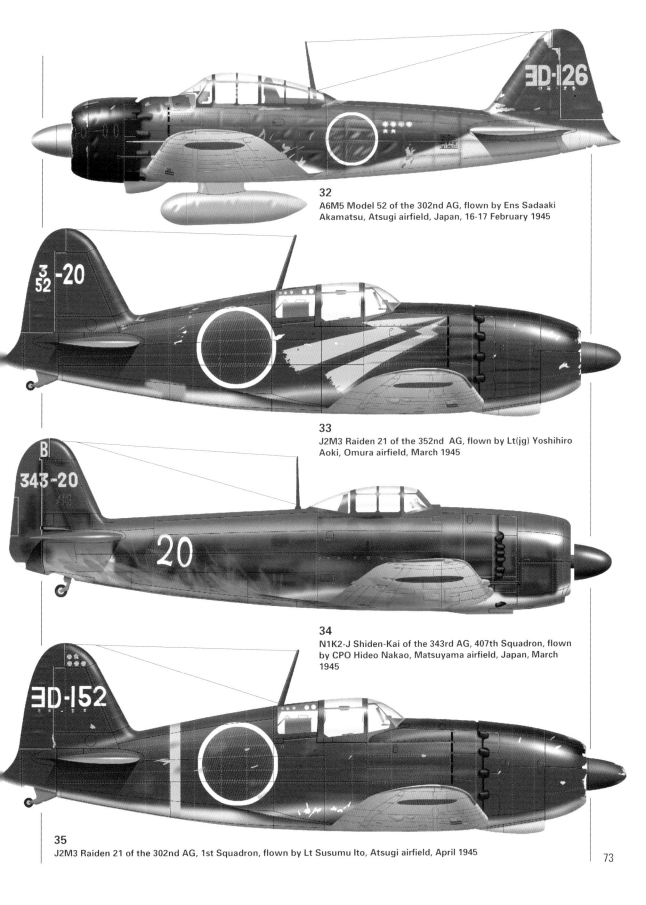

**32**
A6M5 Model 52 of the 302nd AG, flown by Ens Sadaaki
Akamatsu, Atsugi airfield, Japan, 16-17 February 1945

**33**
J2M3 Raiden 21 of the 352nd AG, flown by Lt(jg) Yoshihiro
Aoki, Omura airfield, March 1945

**34**
N1K2-J Shiden-Kai of the 343rd AG, 407th Squadron, flown
by CPO Hideo Nakao, Matsuyama airfield, Japan, March
1945

**35**
J2M3 Raiden 21 of the 302nd AG, 1st Squadron, flown by Lt Susumu Ito, Atsugi airfield, April 1945

**36**
N1K2-J Shiden-Kai 21 of the 343rd AG, 301st Squadron,
flown by CPO Katsue Kato, Matsuyama airfield, April 1945

**37**
J2M3 Raiden 21 of the 332nd AG's Tatsumaki Unit, flown
by WO Susumu Ishihara, Kanoya Air Base, 27 April 1945

**38**
N1K2-J Shiden-Kai 21 of the Yokosuka AG, flown by Ens Kaneyoshi Muto, April 1945

**39**
N1K2-J Shiden-Kai 21 of the 343rd AG, 407th Squadron, flown by WO Isamu Miyazaki, Kyushu, April 1945

**40**
N1K2-J Shiden-Kai 21 of the 343rd AG, 301st Squadron, flown by squadron leader Lt Naoshi Kanno, Matsuyama airfield, Japan, April 1945

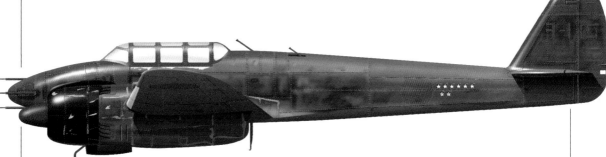

**41**
J1N1-S Gekko Model 23 of the Yokosuka AG, 7th Squadron, flown by CPO Juzo Kuramoto (pilot) and Ens Shiro Kurotori (observer), Yokosuka airfield, May 1945

**42**
A6M5 Model 52 of the 203rd AG, 303rd Squadron, flown by CPO Takeo Tanimizu, Kagoshima Prefecture, Japan, June 1945

**43**
A6M7 Model 63 of the 302nd AG, flown by squadron leader Lt Yutaka Morioka, Atsugi airfield, Japan, 3 August 1945

**1**
PO3/c Sadamu Komachi, serving aboard *Shokaku* in 1941-42

**2**
Lt Yutaka Morioka of the 302nd AG at Atsugi in early 1945

**3**
PO1/c Takeo Tanimizu, serving aboard *Junyo* in May 1942

4
Lt(jg) Sadaaki Akamatsu of the 302nd AG at Atsugi in early 1945

5
PO1/c Kaneyoshi Muto of the 12th AG, formerly in China, in 1938

6
PO2/c Saburo Sakai of the 12th AG at Nanchang, in southern China, in 1939

# HOME DEFENCE

The loss of both the Philippines and Iwo Jima now positioned Allied forces at Japan's 'front door', and it came as no surprise when Saipan-based B-29s raided the Imperial capital for the first time on 24 November 1944.

It was the turn of US carrier aircraft to strike at Tokyo for the first time since Lt Col 'Jimmy' Doolittle surprise raid of 1942 on 16/17 February 1945, TF58 aircraft attacking airfields across the region. In response, the JNAF and JAAF sortied practically anything that could fly – including fixed-landing gear 'relics' from the China War. Both sides once again distorted their results, with combined claims by the JNAF/JAAF amounting to 275 kills against the loss of 78 fighters in the air, whilst the US Navy claimed 330+ victories for 52 F6Fs and 16 F4Us lost to all causes.

Adm Marc Mitscher swung his task force towards southern Japan after 'slapping' Tokyo, his priority now being to destroy airfields in the Kyushu area in order to prevent *kamikaze*s from taking off.

During these 'dark days' when the JNAF suffered defeat after defeat, one unit would shine. Capt Minoru Genda – who masterminded the Pearl Harbor raid – formed an elite unit composed of veterans armed with the latest naval fighter, the Shiden-Kai ('George'). Officially titled the 343rd AG, the group was dubbed the 'Squadron of Experts' because it had the highest concentration of aces of any unit then in the JNAF.

On 19 March 1945 TF58 aircraft took off for an early morning raid against the great naval bastion of Kure, the pilots involved confident in the knowledge that no serious fighter opposition would oppose them. However, Capt Genda scrambled three squadrons of 'Georges', with first contact being made between VBF-17 F6Fs and elements of the 407th and 701st Sqns. A vicious dogfight erupted and six pilots from both sides went down, this action setting the tempo for the morning battles which ranged far and wide. Few fighters from other JNAF/JAAF units joined in due to a lack of fuel – the day belonged to Genda's 343rd.

According to the group's records, they claimed 53 Hellcats and Corsairs and four SB2C Helldivers against a loss of 13 pilots on this day. CPO Katsue Kato alone was credited with nine victories in the morning combat, and these tremendous claims made headlines throughout Japan, temporarily raising morale.

B-29s continued to raid the industrial centres of Japan, however, although the inaccuracy of high altitude bombing forced USAAF commanders to initiate low altitude bombing at night. Devastating fire raids commenced on the night of

Zero pilots of the 203rd AG study their day's assignment at Kagoshima Naval Air Station in May 1945. On the left is CPO Takeo Tanimizu (32 victories), whilst the he pilot on the right has an 8 mm Nambu pistol in his hand (*T Tanimizu*)

Members of the 303rd Squadron, 203rd AG, in July 1945. This unit was reorganised numerous times, and suffered heavy losses over the Philippines, Okinawa and during home defence missions. CPO Takeo Tanimizu (second row, fifth from left) was the most experienced veteran in the group, the majority of his squadronmates having only just graduated from flying school (*T Tanimizu*)

9/10 March, which resulted in nearly 16 square miles of Tokyo being gutted. In response the JNAF sent up teams of 'Gekko' nightfighters, but they achieved marginal results. The most famous B-29 'killer' of them all was Lt Yukio Endo, who had earlier pioneered the art of nightfighting in the Solomons. He and his observer downed at least eight Boeing 'heavies' before they were killed.

Starting in April, P-51s and P-47s began escorting the B-29s over Japan from their bases on Iwo Jima, and Japanese pilots were hard pressed to compete against these menaces. The navy's most famous Mustang 'tamer' was Lt(jg) Sadaaki Akamatsu of the 302nd AG at Atsugi, who proved to the doubters that the Raiden ('Jack') could 'whip' a Mustang by downing at least two in wild dogfight on 19 April. But it was never easy, as Akamatsu observed in a postwar interview;

'I have witnessed so many splendid enemy pilots. It was towards the end of the war when I had one particular encounter with a P-51. We spotted the enemy planes over the southern end of Tokyo Bay. Five Raidens raced in to fight. The enemy always kept their tail covered with the P-51. I hid behind a P-51 – there was a blind spot. After following a while I had the advantage to attack. I fired my guns from very close range and hit its fuel tank. Suddenly it fell on fire. His comrades saw this and spiralled down to attack me. I couldn't escape so I tried a head-on attack. I could see tracers coming toward me, but I was accustomed to this. The enemy never separated me and finally gave up to save fuel. Maybe because it was a hard fight, I respected the enemy's abilities.'

As the war drew to a close, very few JNAF fighters were seen, orders having been given to conserve fuel and fighters for the one big *kamikaze* attack that would greet the anticipated Allied landings.

Aside from lacking fuel, JNAF pilots also felt that their aircraft were by poor. Lt Cdr Iyozoh Fujita was one such individual who had many complaints about the equipment and armament his pilots had to work with;

These A6M5c Zero Model 52s belong to the 252nd AG, and are seen undergoing engine runs prior to their pilots strapping in anticipation of the next home defence sortie. The A6M5c had an additional 13.2 mm machine-gun in each wing, armour plate behind the pilot's seat and a self-sealing fuel tank behind the cockpit. Despite these improvements, the aircraft was still no match for its American fighter opponents (*via Aerospace Publishing*)

'During the early part of the war we felt that the weapons in our Zeroes (two 7.7 mm and 20 mm guns) were adequate, but later on this was not enough. Our pilots wanted 13 and 15 mm guns like the Grummans, but we were unable to have them and I don't know why. Our gunsights were adequate for the veterans, but I requested better ones like those used by the Americans. Again we never received them. I knew about the German Me 262 jet and their rocket fighters. We wanted them too, but couldn't get them.'

The last major dogfight of World War 2 occurred on 15 August 1945 when VF-88 Hellcats encountered a mixed formation of Zeroes and 'Jacks' of the 302nd AG near Atsugi. In a running gunfight, four Hellcats were lost. Two hours later the Emperor broadcast his surrender announcement, but the guns of the JNAF did not remain silent.

On 17 August unescorted B-32 Dominators flew over Tokyo on a photo-reconnaissance mission and were duly intercepted by fighters from the Yokosuka AG. Ens Saburo Sakai and WO Sadamu Komachi chased one bomber to Oshima Island, where it ditched – the loss was recorded as operational. This incident was repeated the following day when the bombers again returned without escorts – this time one B-32 crewman was killed in the attacks, Sgt Anthony J Marchione dying aboard the 312th BG's *Hobo Queen*.

Saburo Sakai explained the rationale for their actions in the following quote;

'It may appear that we committed an illegal act. I investigated this matter after the war. What we did was perfectly legal and acceptable under international law and the rules of engagement. While Japan did agree to the surrender, we were still a sovereign nation, and every nation has the right to protect itself. When the Americans sent over their B-32s, we did not know of their intentions . . . By invading our airspace they were committing a provocative and aggressive act . . . It was most unwise for the Americans to send over their bombers only a few days after the surrender announcement! They should have waited and let things cool down.'

Many Japanese pilots, believing a rumour that the US occupation forces had plans to execute them in reprisal, burned their logbooks, while executive officers destroyed mission reports and other data. In this fashion, much detailed information on units and pilots was lost to history.

# Warrant Officer Takeo Tanimizu

'I believe in fate. God determines at the time of birth just when and where a person shall die', recalled Takeo Tanimizu, a truly remarkable fighter ace whose specially-marked Zero is the most easily recognisable of its type due to its unique kill markings.

Tanimizu was born in Mie Prefecture in April 1919, his mother being a pearl diver. He too followed aquatic pursuits by joining the navy – against the wishes of his mother – when the Pacific War started, entering flight training and duly graduating in March 1942. After various assignments (none involving combat), Tanimizu transferred to the *Shokaku* in February 1943. However, it wasn't until 2 November 1943 at Rabaul that he finally engaged the enemy, claiming two P-38s in his first combat.

The daily battles over Rabaul took a tremendous toll of Zero pilots, with Tanimizu considering the Hellcat to be his greatest foe;

'I think the F6F was the toughest opponent we had. They could manoeuvre and roll, whereas planes such as the P-38 and F4U made hit and run passes – they were not very manoeuvrable. It was difficult to make the American planes burn in the air. If you hit them, they may puff some smoke. You could always tell by the way they smoked if it was a Zero or an enemy plane.'

The gull-winged F4U had a ferocious reputation amongst the Americans, who nicknamed it 'Whistling Death'. However, although most

CPO Takeo Tanimizu painted elaborate kill markings on his Zero 03-09 in an effort to bolster the morale of his men. The stars with arrows through them indicate a sure victory, while the single marking below is a probable. His scoreboard also boasted two head-on silhouettes of B-29s, although these are obscured in this photograph by the sun's reflection. This shot was taken in June 1945 in Kyushu (*T Tanimizu*)

In 1945 the 352nd AG flew Raiden ('Jack') fighters against B-29s over western Kyushu from their base at Kanoya. Although the unit trained to use deadly aerial burst bombs, no victories were achieved with the weapon. JNAF ace Lt Yoshihiro Aoki (second from left) is seen briefing his men before a mission in front of his distinctively marked 'Jack' (*K Osuo*)

Zero pilots respected the Corsair, they did not fear it. Tanimizu recalled;

'The only time you could really shoot it down was when it was fleeing. You had to shoot at it from a certain angle, otherwise, the bullets would bounce off. A few times, I would see F4U making low level diving attacks and dive into a coconut grove or the water because it couldn't pull out – the plane was too heavy. We would sometimes chase them into the sea. We didn't have this problem because our planes were so light.'

Despite the 'kill or be killed' philosophy, Tanimizu also showed compassion for the enemy. On 4 January 1944, while returning from combat, he saw a lone Corsair pilot parachute from his damaged aircraft into the waters off Capt St George. Concerned for his opponent, Tanimizu flew down and threw Capt Harvey F Carter of VMF-321 his life ring. Carter retrieved the ring and waved thanks to his foe, but was never recovered.

In March 1944 Tanimizu became an instructor with the Tainan AG in

A Kawanishi N1K Kyofu ('Rex') floatplane of the Sasebo AG flies over Kyushu in September 1944. The Shiden and Shiden-Kai fighters were developed from this advanced, yet temperamental floatplane, of which only 97 were built (*via Aerospace Publishing*)

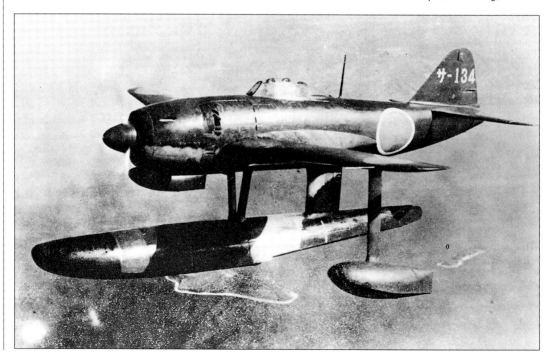

The pilot of an unidentified N1K1-J runs the aircraft's unreliable Nakajima Homare 21 powerplant up on the ramp whilst his mechanics examine the fighter's undercarriage legs – another of the fighter's problem areas (*via Robert C Mikesh*)

The 'George' was a direct descendant of the 'Rex' floatplane, the 201st AG taking it to the Philippines, where it held its own against the F6F Hellcat (*via Phil Jarrett*)

Japan, although shortly afterwards he was sent to Formosa to perform bomber intercepts and general patrol duties. He also very occasionally flew nocturnal sorties, and on the night of 31 August 1944, he engaged 11 B-24s attacking Takao (now Kaohsiung) Harbour by himself. Tanimizu made frontal passes on a B-24 piloted by Lt Norman B Clendenen of the 425th BS, causing the Liberator crash in flames – there was only one survivor, who was duly captured. He may also have damaged the bomber flown by Lt George Pierpont, the B-24 crashing into a mountain peak on mainland China. The remains of the crew were only discovered in October 1996, being handed over to the US Ambassador in January 1997.

On 3 November 1944, over Amoy Harbour (China), Tanimizu and his

wingman, Manabu Ito, had commenced their landing approach after providing air cover for a convoy of ships entering the harbour when they were bounced by two P-51s of the 74th FS flown by Capt Paul J Reis and 1Lt John W Bolyard. Firing from extreme distance, Reis hit Tanimizu's wing tip, but the ace failed to see the closing Mustangs, assuming instead that his inexperienced wingman trailing behind him had accidentally fired a burst. Bolyard quickly downed Ito and flamed Tanimizu's A6M (these were the Mustang pilot's first in an eventual tally of five kills).

'My Zero was out of control, on fire, and going straight up', he later recalled, 'and then I thought, "so this is where I am going to die!"'

Tanimizu managed to extricate himself from the burning aircraft and parachuted at just 250 ft, his 'chute opening just before he hit the water. He was eventually rescued by two Chinese from a nearby beach nearly two hours later.

The later N1K2-J Shiden-Kai (with its repositioned wing and lengthened fuselage) was a vast improvement on the original Shiden (*via Phil Jarrett*)

Raiden fighters of the 1st Squadron, 302nd AG, are seen at Atsugi in 1945 – note that the three fighters in the second row all sport kill markings on their tails. Designed to attack B-29s, the 'Jack' and was not a particularly manoeuvrable aircraft, and most pilots disliked it due to its heavy handling and excessive landing speed. However, Ens Sadaaki Akamatsu – and a few others – was able to outfight P-51s in the aircraft

A 302nd AG Raiden scrambles to intercept an incoming raid. Operating a mixed force of both Zeroes and 'Jacks' from Atsugi airfield, the unit was the guardian of the Imperial Capital. However, by May 1945, the 302nd was down to just ten operational aircraft, and it flew its last combat mission on 15 August 1945 – two hours before the surrender announcement – when Hellcats from VF-88 were engaged (*via Aerospace Publishing*)

The 'Jack' was a pugnacious looking design when viewed from almost any angle (*via Aerospace Publishing*)

After spending a month in a hospital in Formosa, Tanimizu was ordered back to Japan, where his request for a *kamikaze* assignment was rejected by an admiral – he was sent instead to the 203rd AG in Kyushu.

On 18 March 1945 Tanimizu fought Corsairs which were strafing his airfield at Kasanbara, shooting one off the tail of a comrade and inflicting serious damage on another, flown by Lt James J Stevens of VBF-83. Stevens fled at low altitude over the sea, trailing a plume of black smoke, and although Tanimizu tried to chase him down, he failed to catch him. The F4U had been fatally wounded, however, Stevens subsequently drowning after ditching his aircraft.

To give the inexperienced pilots in his unit confidence, Tanimizu began applying victory markings to his aircraft. One was for the F4U downed over Kasanbara, whilst others denoted a B-29 shared with Ens Tetsuzo Iwamoto (the top JNAF ace) and a second as a probable.

This candid shot shows a wrestling match underway in a corner of Atsugi airfield in early 1945. Ens Sadaaki Akamatsu (second from left, without a flying helmet) was a champion wrestler, in addition to being a renowned ace (*Sakaida*)

On 10 June 1945 Tanimizu fought against P-47s in a savage battle over Kyushu, and although he seriously damaged a Thunderbolt, his Zero was hit in the oil pipe and he was forced to make an emergency landing.

When the surrender was announced on 15 August 1945 Tanimizu could not accept defeat. For five days, he searched for enemy aircraft and dropped leaflets urging the public to fight on.

By the end of the war Takeo Tanimizu had recorded 1425 flight hours and claimed 32 victories. He is now retired and resides in Osaka.

## Lieutenant(jg) Sadaaki Akamatsu

'Outrageously temperamental, eccentric and quite violent!' were the words used by ace Saburo Sakai to describe this fighter pilot. Temei (he preferred this nickname to the formal Sadaaki) Akamatsu was the JNAF's most infamous fighter ace, whose antics became legendary.

Born in Kochi Prefecture in July 1910, the son of a weatherman, Akamatsu entered the navy in June 1928, commenced flight training two years later and graduated in March 1932. The high quality of the prewar training instilled in each pilot an extreme sense of self-confidence, and honed the killer instinct – traits which helped Akamatsu survive the war.

Following the completion of his training, Akamatsu (his name means red pine) served with various air groups, including those on the carriers *Akagi*, *Ryujo* and *Kaga*. When the China War commenced in 1937, he was transferred to the 13th AG and went into combat.

The rogue fighter pilot known as 'Matsu-chan' (little pine) was good from the very start, for on 25 February 1938, during his first action over Nanchang, he claimed four enemy aircraft shot down. In September he transferred to *Soryu* Fighter Squadron. The vicious engagements of the China War helped hone Akamatsu's fighting style to the point where he would take the offensive even when facing a numerically superior enemy.

Ens Sadaaki Akamatsu, the JNAF's top Raiden master, demonstrates how to attack an American fighter. He never lost a dogfight in more than eight years of combat, and ended the war without having suffered as much as a scratch (*Sakaida*)

At the end of his combat tour in China, Akamatsu returned to Japan as a war hero. 'I destroyed over 200 enemy aircraft including confirmed, probables and burned on the ground', he recalled in his postwar years. 'The time before World War 2, the fighter plane didn't have the great speeds; it was the pilot's ability that counted. It was the "one-to-one dog-fight era". The fight was slower and determined; we didn't fight in massed formations.'

The self-proclaimed 'King of Aces' earned a notorious reputation as an undisciplined rebel and womaniser, and it was no secret that he was also an alcoholic. His heavy drinking and violent temper often resulted in fights, landing him in the brig. Despite having his service stripes taken away and being held back in rank, Akamatsu was nevertheless respected by his subordinates for his fighting ability, and tolerated by his superiors.

When Japan went to war on 8 December 1941, WO Akamatsu flew with the 3rd AG on a raid against Iba and Clark Fields, where he fought against 20th PS P-40s and claimed one damaged. Two days later he shared a victory over Manila with two other pilots.

From the Philippines, the 3rd AG fought over the Dutch East Indies, where, according to Akamatsu's recollections, he downed two 'Curtiss Nieuports' over Surabaya, Java, and also shared in the destruction of a fly-ing boat with two other pilots. Over Bali, two more P-40s fell to his guns, and when his unit attacked Darwin (Australia) from their base at Kupang, Akamatsu added a single Spitfire to his tally. It wasn't until May 1942 that the veteran ace returned to Japan.

In July 1943, Ens Akamatsu was posted to the 331st AG, with whom he fought over Calcutta and claimed four enemy aircraft shot down on 5 December 1943. The following month Akamatsu returned to Japan and was assigned to the tough 302nd AG at Atsugi airfield, where he became a division officer within a Raiden ('Jack') unit. His new job brought many responsibilities with it, and he mended his evil ways except for his drink-ing. The old master trained his young subordinates to respect enemy fighters – 'Use hit and run attacks', Akamatsu would advise his men. 'The American pilots have excellent radio communications and group tactics'.

When American carrier fighters raided the Tokyo region on 16 Febru-ary 1945, Ens Akamatsu jumped into a Zero and plunged into the Hell-cat formations. He downed two in the morning sortie and another pair in the afternoon, and by war's end, he had accounted for nine F6Fs (four confirmed and five probables).

Akamatsu's fighting ability reached legendary status with his handling of the J2M Raiden fighter. The aircraft had initially been designed as a bomber interceptor, and was widely despised by navy pilots, who com-plained constantly about its lack of manoeuvrability, high landing speed and oversized cowling. It was often mistaken for the enemy's P-47 Thun-derbolt, and there was a high accident rate amongst trainees. Many vet-eran pilots believed that this aircraft could not survive against Hellcats and Mustangs in a dogfight.

Ens Akamatsu was not intimidated by the American aircraft, however, stating, 'Our dogfighting techniques were superior to any other coun-try's, but the American's shooting average was better than ours.'

In an astonishing display of aerobatics and raw courage, Akamatsu proved that a Raiden could break a Mustang when, on 19 April 1945, the

34-year-old 'Raiden Master' flew his 'Jack' against P-51s of the 45th FS. Fighting on his own terms, he forced his opponents down to low altitude and claimed two or three shot down.

On 29 May, near Yokohama, the 'old man' of the Atsugi Air Corps single-handedly attacked 75 Mustangs in a Zero and shot down 2Lt Rufus Moore, again of the 45th FS. Capt Todd Moore, who witnessed Akamatsu's attack, said later, 'If he had been an American he would have been awarded the Congressional Medal of Honor'.

When the surrender announcement was broadcast by the Emperor on 15 August 1945, Lt(jg) Akamatsu sided with the faction at Atsugi who vowed to continue fighting. However, the air group's fighters were disabled and the rebellion was quashed.

Akamatsu ended his flying career with more than 8000 flight hours, and he often boasted of over 350 victories when he was intoxicated and 260 when he was sober, but almost no one believed him. In addition to the nine F6F Hellcats that he claimed, several Mustangs, one B-24 and seven B-29s (one confirmed and six probables) also appear in his victory list. According to available records, and his peers, he probably scored over 30 victories, and although his fighter was hit many times, Akamatsu was never wounded.

It was only natural that such a 'character' who defied the odds and survived would achieve legendary status within the ranks of the JNAF. Akamatsu was said to have engaged in combat while in a drunken stupor, whilst another story concerning his exploits had the nonconformist bolting from a brothel during an air raid and jumping into his fighter still wearing his kimono and wooden clogs! Saburo Sakai, who knew Akamatsu, replied, 'Don't believe those silly stories – it's all nonsense!'

The postwar years proved difficult for the alcoholic ex-fighter pilot. His old comrades took up a collection and presented him with a small Piper, which he flew as a fish search pilot for the Kochi Fishery Association until he eventually sold it to keep himself in drink. Ruined in health by his alcoholism and ostracised by his friends and former comrades, he ran a small cafe in Kochi City until he died on 22 February 1980 of pneumonia, a broken and dejected man.

## Lieutenant Yukio Endo

Yukio Endo was regarded as the navy's top B-29 'killer', his pioneering efforts in nightfighting helping the JNAF to develop tactics that enabled fighters to engage the previously invincible B-29s over Japan.

Born in Yamagata Prefecture in September 1915, the future 'King of B-29 Killers' graduated from flight training in 1933 and went on to become a carrier pilot. Endo flew ground support missions in 1938 during the China War, but failed to score any aerial victories before returning to the homeland and becoming an instructor. This tasking lasted until January 1943, when he was assigned to the 251st AG.

USAAC B-17s from Port Moresby had been pounding Rabaul during their nocturnal sorties with near impunity, the crews considering their missions as mere 'milk runs' due to the inaccuracy of anti-aircraft fire. Cdr Yasuna Kozono, CO of the 251st AG, formulated a plan to counter the Flying Fortresses by arming a twin-engined aircraft with a pair of

Lt Yukio Endo was JNAF's top B-29 'killer' who, having perfected methods of attacking the Superfortress in combat, trained other teams in nightfighting tactics (*K Osuo*)

obliquely-mounted 20 mm cannons, the eccentric, hot-headed, commander forcing his plan into action despite being ridiculed by most of his peers and superiors. Lt(jg) Endo was picked by Kozono to test the first model of the Gekko ('Irving').

When the commander's new weapon made its combat debut, the honour of downing the first B-17 in a night action over Rabaul fell to PO1/c Shigetoshi Kudo on 21 May 1943 – despite repeated sorties, Endo failed to score, while his comrades succeeded in spectacular fashion. He returned to Japan and was assigned to the 302nd AG at Atsugi in March 1944, where his job was to train more Gekko nightfighter crews in anticipation of American bombing raids over the mainland.

When Twentieth Air Force B-29s bombed Japan for the first time on the night of 15/16 June 1944, Lt(jg) Endo transferred to the 352nd AG, based at Omura airfield in Kyushu. With eight fully-trained flight crews, he was anxious to put his men to the test, and on the night of 20 August 88 B-29s raided northern Kyushu and his men sortied in force – in one of the costliest missions of the war, the USAAF lost 14 B-29s to all causes.

Endo succeeded in aligning his aircraft beneath the tail of a B-29 over Sasebo, and with calm precision, proceeded to rake the undersides of the Superfortress, which fell away in flames. He repeated this manoeuvre and heavily damaged another, and by the time Endo had finally finished his mission, his tally stood at two destroyed, one probable and two damaged.

From his first encounter with B-29s until his death, Lt(jg) Endo flew night and day intercept missions, returning to Atsugi in November 1944. On 14 January 1945 Yukio Endo intercepted a daylight raid performed by 73rd BW B-29s on Nagoya. After he had shot down one bomber and damaged another, his aircraft was hit and burst into flames. His observer, WO Osamu Nishio, attempted to parachute to safety but failed to survive, whilst Endo, who had been badly burned trying to control the Gekko, attempted to parachute at low altitude but was killed.

A posthumous citation issued to the team of Endo and Nishio on 11 February 1945 by Adm Funizo Tsukahara, CO of the Yokosuka Naval Station stated;

'You downed eight B-29s and damaged more than eight others with your nightfighter when they came over Nagoya and Tokyo. You intercepted the B-29s over the area piloting a nightfighter of the 302nd AG with high more morale and distinguished skills. You are hereby cited.'

He was promoted two ranks to commander.

## Chief Petty Officer Shoichi Sugita

Shoichi Sugita became the top ace of the 204th AG during the Solomons campaign, and was one of the JNAF's five highest scoring pilots. He was born in 1924 in Niigata Prefecture, and at the age of 15, dropped out of agriculture school and joined the Imperial Navy.

In March 1942 Sugita graduated from flight training and arrived at his new base at Buin in October. In his first combat on 1 December 1942, he teamed with up PO2/c Saji Kanda to destroy a B-17 over the airfield, although in the process he struck the bomber with his right wing but nevertheless managed to land safely. On the 28th Sugita shared in the destruction of another B-17 over Buin.

Lt Takashi Oshibuchi was a great fighter-leader who fought with the 201st and 253rd AGs at Rabaul, before being given command of the 701st Squadron of the 343rd AG. Oshibuchi was killed on 24 July 1945 over the Bungo Straits by VF-49 Hellcats, his score at the time standing at six victories (*Sakaida*)

The 301st Squadron of the 343rd AG is seen at Matsuyama Airfield in March 1945, this outfit boasting the highest number of aces of any air group at this time. Sitting in the front row (centre) is Capt Minoru Genda, the mastermind of the Pearl Harbor attack and CO of the unit. Lt Naoshi Kanno (48 victories) is in the front row, second from left, whilst the top ace of the unit, CPO Shoichi Sugita (120+ kills), is third from right in the second row. To Sugita's right is CPO Tomoichi Kasai (10 victories) (*Y Izawa*)

CPO Shoichi Sugita claimed two P-38s on the ill-fated Adm Yamamoto escort mission of April 1943. He was an extremely aggressive pilot to the point of being reckless, and it was this trait that eventually led him to his death on 15 April 1945 over Kanoya airfield (*Maru*)

On 2 January 1943 he fought with Wildcats of VMF-121 over Munda Point and claimed one shot down (two were lost). Before month's end, he had claimed another three F4Fs and shared in the destruction of a B-24.

On 18 April Sugita was one of six Zero pilots selected to fly as escort for two 'Betty' bombers, one carrying Adm Isoroku Yamamoto, Commander in Chief of the Combined Fleet. They were ambushed by P-38s and the two bombers shot down. In the wild dogfight that followed, Sugita hit and damaged a P-38 flown by 1Lt Raymond K Hine and may have shot him down (he was the only American lost on this mission). However, his claim for two P-38s was a hollow victory, for each pilot blamed himself for their collective failure to protect their distinguished leader.

Given every chance to redeem their honour by death in combat, the escort pilots threw all caution to the wind, and within three months four of them were dead, and the fifth, Kenji Yanagiya, had been seriously wounded and sent back to Japan. However, instead of embracing death, sole survivor Sugita relished the increasing levels of combat, honing his already razor sharp fighting skills to the point where he became the deadliest of foes.

Sugita claimed Corsairs for the first time on 12 June when he engaged VMF-112 over Guadalcanal. He downed one and shared another, and four days later claimed another F4U (from VMF-122). Sugita's final F4U kill came on 25 August. Just 24 hours later the Marines got their revenge when Sugita was hit by Corsairs from either VMF-214 or -215 south-east of the Shortlands. Forced to bale out with serious burns, he was sent back to Japan.

In March 1944 Sugita joined the 263rd AG and saw heavy action in the Carolines and Marianas. On 8 July he was in a flight of six Zeroes (led by Lt Yasuhiro Shigematsu – group leader with 10+ victories) on their way to Palau that was overwhelmed by VF-31 Hellcats near Yap. All bar Sugita were shot down, and he barely escaped to Peleliu. Leaderless, and with only a handful of aircraft on Guam, the unit was disbanded ten days later and Sugita and a handful of survivors escaped north to the Philippines.

His next assignment was with the 201st AG in the Philippines. Once again he was in constant combat, claiming victory after victory while his comrades fell all around him, and by the time he returned to Japan in January 1945 he had claimed over 120 kills.

An elite fighter air group was formed by Capt Minoru Genda in December 1944 at Matsuyama, on Shikoku Island, the unit being armed exclusively with the new Shiden-Kai ('George'). Genda personally selected Sugita to be a member, and upon his arrival he was posted to the 301st Squadron. In the unit's first combat on 19 March 1945 over Kure, Sugita and his flight claimed three Hellcats.

CPO Shoichi Sugita finally met death on 15 April 1945. American carrier aircraft raided airfields in Kyushu in an effort to destroy *kamikaze* suicide aircraft which posed a serious threat to American warships in Okinawan waters. VF-46's Lt Cdr Robert 'Doc' Weatherup led his strike group in an attack on Kanoya airfield, and when the Hellcats were seen approaching, Sugita and his wingman, PO2/c Toyomi Miyazawa, ran towards two fighters being prepared for take-off at one end of the flightline. Ens Saburo Sakai yelled at Sugita to take cover, but his warning was ignored, and struggling to build up speed as he climbed through 200 ft, he met his end.

Lt Cdr Weatherup, who had completed his rocket and strafing attack on an aircraft in a revetment, then spotted Sugita taking off. He circled around, pulled a big lead, and waited until the wingspan of the ace's fighter was 35 mils in his sight, then opened fire. Sugita apparently saw the tracers and tried to relax his turn, but it was too late. Weatherup saw flicks where his 'slugs' were hitting armour, then the 'George' nosed over trailing a thin plume of smoke. It crashed in a ball of fire at the end of the airfield, and seconds later Weatherup consigned Miyazawa to a similar fate.

In a personal citation issued to Sugita posthumously on 1 August 1945, he was recognised as having achieved 70 individual and 40 shared victories. Since Capt Genda would not accord Sugita a double rank promotion for distinguished service (he reserved such honours for officers), higher authorities intervened and Shoichi Sugita was duly promoted to ensign.

In May 1982, Saburo Sakai met Robert Weatherup at a reunion in California. 'I was looking up from the air raid shelter when I saw you shoot down my comrade', said Sakai. 'He was a great ace but a little reckless.' The two shook hands in the spirit of friendship, and commented on the loss of a great airman.

An unidentified pilot of the 407th Squadron, 343rd AG, stands by the tail of Shiden-Kai 343-B-03, flown by ace WO Koji Ohara. Of interest is the white '03' just visible in the 'meat-ball', which was used for training purposes. The small white box on the tail reads '2 Suzuki', which translates to 'Section 2, Suzuki', denoting the aircraft's maintainer. The wooden brace across its tail was used to secure the rudder, thus protecting it from wind damage during violent storms (*Y Shiga*)

CPO Hideo Nakao takes a break on the tail of 343-B-20, a Shiden-Kai of the 407th Squadron of the 343rd AG. The white maintenance assignment box reads 'Section 4 Ochiai' (top), 'Kitagawa' (left), and 'Nakao' (right). Ochiai was the chief mechanic for this aircraft, followed by Kitagawa and Nakao (not related to the pilot). CPO Nakao claimed an F6F on 19 March 1945, followed several months later by a P-51 (*K Osuo*)

WO Katsue Kato was a rare 'double ace-in-a-day', achieving the feat during the 343rd AG's baptism of fire on 19 March 1945. Although he claimed ten kills, his tally was never officially recognised (*K Osuo*)

Lt Naoshi Kanno is seen posing in front of a Zero 21 in 1943 at Oita airfield. Although his 'gung ho' fighting spirit endeared him to his CO, Capt Genda, a number of his men felt that he was reckless (*Y Ikari*)

## Warrant Officer Katsue Kato

Katsue Kato became a rare 'ace-in-a-day' while flying the new Shiden-Kai with the 'Squadron of Experts'. Born in March 1924 in Ibaragi Prefecture, young Katsue entered naval flight training in October 1941 at Tsuchiura. Graduating in January 1943, he began specialised training as a seaplane pilot. however, due to the tremendous demand for fighter pilots in the Solomons, Kato switched courses, and after a brief training period, was assigned firstly to the 381st AG, then to the 311th Squadron of the 153rd AG. He advanced with the latter group to western New Guinea, where he participated in combat over Biak. At the end of 1944, Kato returned to Japan and was selected to join the 343rd AG.

When US Navy carrier fighters raided Kure Harbour on 19 March 1945, Kato hurled himself into the massed ranks of F6Fs as the No 3 wingman to Lt Naoshi Kanno, CO of the 301st Squadron. By morning's end, he had claimed a record nine destroyed, but because the dogfights were conducted by formations, Kato's individual score was not announced, nor officially recognised. However, his performance was so outstanding that he was cited in the Naval All Units Proclamation.

On 16 April 1945 CPO Katsue Kato was killed in aerial combat with more F6F Hellcats (from VF-17) over Amami Island. It is uncertain whether his score was in excess of nine kills at the time of his death.

## Lieutenant Naoshi Kanno

The Naval Academy's top ace, Naoshi Kanno was born on 13 October 1921 in Miyagi Prefecture. Upon graduation from the Etajima academy in the Class of 70 in December 1941, he entered flight training and became a fighter pilot in September 1943.

Kanno first taste of combat came in April 1944 when he was sent to Micronesia as a division officer for the original 343rd AG, remaining with the unit until it was disbanded on 10 July due to combat losses. He was next transferred to the 306th Squadron of the 201st AG, where he gained considerable fame for his combat prowess.

One of his much-admired tactics saw him fearlessly attacking B-24s, sent to bomb Yap Island, from head-on – while still perfecting his technique, Kanno rammed a Liberator and damaged it, but still managed to survive. His squadron claimed over 60 aircraft destroyed around Yap in July, for which it received a unit citation.

In October 1944 the *kamikaze* corps was formed in the Philippines, and it was widely believed that Lt Kanno would be given the honour of leading it. However, command went to Lt Yukio Seki (another Naval Academy graduate), for Kanno was in Japan procuring aircraft for his unit at the time.

When the 343rd AG was reorganised for the second time, Kanno was given command of the 301st Squadron. The unit was now equipped with the Shiden-Kai ('George') fighters, which were Japan's answer to the Hellcat. In their baptism of fire over Japan, the 343rd intercepted carrier aircraft attacking targets in Kure Harbour on 19 March 1945, the 301st initially engaging F4Us of VMF-123 north of Kure Naval Base, before various divisions became separated as the morning combat raged on.

After a wild dogfight off the eastern coast of Shikoku Island, Lt Kanno reassembled his men to resume the hunt. Within minutes a pair of VBF-10 F4Us, flown by Lt Robert 'Windy' Hill and Ens Roy D Erickson, encountered the 'Georges' from astern, the former pilot squeezing off a burst at the leader who was flying straight and level. Lt Kanno's fighter burst into flames, and the pilot baled out close enough for Erickson to see his astonished face, and his brand new brown flightsuit!

Lt Kanno landed roughly in a farm field not far from Matsuyama Castle, suffering burns to his face and hands. An elderly farmer, mistaking him for an American, advanced on the pilot with a pitchfork, although he soon backed off upon hearing curses aimed at him in Japanese! Quickly appropriating a bicycle, Kanno pedalled furiously back to base.

On 1 August 1945, whilst leading his men against B-24s over Yaku Island, one of his 20 mm cannons blew up due to a mechanical defect, leaving a large hole in his wing. He experienced difficulties in controlling his aircraft and his wingman, WO Mitsuo Hori, offered to stay with him. Kanno kept pointing at the bombers, and when Hori insisted on flying escort, Kanno glared at him and gestured again. The wingman reluctantly left and Kanno was never seen again.

Lt Naoshi Kanno was elevated two ranks to commander and received a posthumous commendation. His bulldog tenacity, while admired by his CO, Capt Genda, worried his subordinates, with some of his men even considering him reckless and overrated. Indeed, of the four squadrons within the 343rd, Kanno's 301st suffered the heaviest casualties.

According to the Naval All Units Proclamation No 214, Kanno had destroyed or damaged 30 enemy aircraft in his combat tour of the Carolines and the Philippines. Additionally, it stated that he achieved another 18 victories while serving with the 343rd, including two B-24s downed on his last mission.

## Ensign Kaneyoshi Muto

'Muto was the toughest fighter pilot in the Imperial Navy!' according to comrade Saburo Sakai. That a man so short in height could wield a Zero fighter like a Samurai sword to 'cut down' far bigger opponents with speed and grace is hard to imagine. Yet Muto was likened to Japan's most famous medieval swordsman, Miyamoto Musashi.

Kaneyoshi Muto (his given name could also be pronounced Kinsuke, which he preferred) was born in June 1916 in Aichi Prefecture to a poor farming family. In June 1935 Muto enlisted in the navy at Kure and briefly served aboard the destroyer *Uranami*. Realising that the aviation service offered career advancement, he applied for, and was accepted into, the flight training programme, graduating in July 1936 and being posted to the Omura AG.

With the advent of the China War, Muto found himself in combat with the 12th AG, scoring his first victory – a Soviet I-16 – over Nanking on 4 December 1937. He fought continuously over Hankow and added four more kills before his tour of duty ended. On 30 April 1938 Muto received a rare official commendation for distinguished service.

When the Pacific War broke out, Muto was a member of the 3rd AG. After attacking Iba and Clark Fields with the group in the first days of

Ens Kaneyoshi Muto was considered the 'toughest pilot in the JNAF' by famed ace Saburo Sakai. Although only 5 ft 3 in tall, he was a 'giant' amongst JNAF aces. Muto was also known for his great sense of humour, which made him a favourite with his comrades (*Y Shiga*)

conflict, he ranged over the Dutch East Indies with the unit. However, the end of the Malayan campaign in April 1942 saw him return to Japan.

In November 1942, Muto advanced to Rabaul with the 252nd AG, subsequently participating in the heavy fighting over the Solomons and eastern New Guinea. In April 1943 he received a military decoration for distinguished service.

In November, 'Kin-Chan' (the nickname means 'Little Gold') was transferred back to the mainland to join the Yokosuka AG, with whom he flew as an instructor with old China War comrade, Saburo Sakai. By the summer of 1944 the war situation had deteriorated to the point where the Yokosuka AG – the proud guardian of the Imperial capital – was ordered to Iwo Jima. On 24 June, the island was attacked by Hellcats, and in a staggeringly one-sided combat, the Americans butchered the Zeroes. Muto, however, returned alive with several victories to his credit. In desperation, he and his men were ordered to crash their aircraft in a *kamikaze* style attack on American warships, Muto and two wingman duly launching on their one-way mission on 5 July. Inbound to the target, they were bounced by Hellcats, forcing them to abort their mission and fight their way back to base. The remnants of the unit were evacuated back to Japan shortly afterwards

Upon his return, Muto was assigned air defence duties over Tokyo, and when B-29s started to bomb Japan in November, he tackled the massed formations of four-engined 'heavies' with typical gusto.

On 16 February 1945 the US Navy launched its first carrier raid against the Tokyo area, and Muto, piloting a new Shiden-Kai ('George') from the

Waiting to sortie, WO Yuzaburo Toguchi (left) and Ens Matsuo Hagiri (13 victories, right) relax at Yokosuka airfield's ready area in 1945. Hagiri claimed an F6F Hellcat during the big carrier raid of 16 February 1945 (*M Hagiri*)

evaluation department of his air group, joined his squadronmates in their efforts to thwart the raiders. Muto became embroiled in a fierce dogfight with F6Fs from VF-82 that saw four Hellcats downed.

Desperate to find heroes to help deflect news of the seemingly endless series of military defeats, the Japanese press found WO Kaneyoshi Muto's deeds during this sortie ideal for their propaganda purposes. An exaggerated version of the combat was duly spread that saw Muto single-handedly take on 12 F6Fs, destroying four – this myth survives to this day.

In June Muto was transferred to the 301st Squadron of the 343rd AG as a replacement pilot for the great ace, Shoichi Sugita, who had been killed in April. On 24 July, during his first combat mission with the unit, Muto failed to return from the Bungo Straits. The squadron's mission on this day was to destroy enemy aircraft heading to their carriers after they had attacked warships anchored in Kure Harbour.

Subsequent research in the 1980s revealed that Muto's flight bounced a pair of VBF-1 F4U Corsairs lagging behind a larger group, swiftly shooting down Ens Robert J Speckman and leaving Lt(jg) Robert Applegate to engage the enemy alone. Just as he was on the verge of being overwhelmed, two Hellcats from VF-88 (flown by Lt Malcolm Cagle and his wingman, Lt(jg) Ken Neyer) charged in to help the lone Corsair pilot. Neyer was also shot down, however, leaving the two surviving Americans to fight their way back to their carrier. Applegate was also eventually shot down, parachuting from his damaged Corsair and subsequently being rescued, leaving Cagle as the only pilot to make it back to his ship.

During the action both Applegate and Cagle had downed three 'Georges', one of which was flown by Muto – it is not known which of them shot down the great ace.

Kaneyoshi Muto received a posthumous promotion to ensign. His final tally of kills cannot be ascertained, for some Japanese historians have estimated his score to be around 28, while others have pegged it at 35.

## Lieutenant Yutaka Morioka

Slim of build and gentle in character, Yutaka Morioka was a fearless fighter-leader and a late starter in the Zero fighter. He was born on 8 March 1922 to parents whose job was guns and explosives distribution.

Morioka entered the Naval Academy at Etajima and graduated on 11 November 1941 in the 70th Class, after which he trained as a 'Val' dive-bomber pilot, but did not see any combat. He subsequently became a dive-bomber instructor with the Usa AG in northern Kyushu.

When the war situation became critical, Morioka was offered the chance to become a Zero pilot, and in April 1944, as a member of the 302nd AG at Atsugi, he began the conversion with the help of the unit's top fighter ace, Ens Sadaaki Akamatsu. In their first dogfighting session, the master instructor and the eager neophyte engaged in mock dogfights over Atsugi airfield until, after about ten minutes, Akamatsu called over the radio, 'Lt Morioka! I have shot you down four times already!' However, after two months of intensive training Akamatsu presented his pupil with a diploma.

In the wake of his conversion, Lt Morioka became the youngest JNAF squadron leader at age 23 when he was given command of three

95

Pilots of the 2nd Squadron, 302nd AG, pose for a group shot at Atsugi airfield in late 1944. The squadron CO, Lt Yutaka Morioka, is seated in the front row, centre – his wingmen on the squadron's final wartime combat mission of 15 August 1945, being Ens Mitsuo Tsuruta (second row, third from right), Ens Muneaki Morimoto (first row, second from left) and Ens Tooru Miyaki (first row, third from right) (*Y Morioka*)

squadrons – two equipped with Raidens and one with Zeroes. From November 1944 onwards, they intercepted B-29s over Tokyo and surrounding areas.

On 23 January 1945 Morioka attacked B-29s of the 73rd BW near Nagoya, damaging a Superfortress before its tail gunner shot off his left hand – his comrades later destroyed the crippled bomber. After brief hospitalisation, Lt Morioka was fitted with an iron claw and returned to combat.

Lt Morioka became an ace just two hours before the end of World War 2 when he shot down a Hellcat from VF-88. He is seen here in the cockpit of his Zero 52, his iron claw clutching the throttle (just visible through the windscreen) (*Y Morioka*)

On 3 August 1945 Morioka led four Zeroes in an attempt to thwart the rescue of Capt Edward Mikes Jr of the 458th FS, who had parachuted from his damaged P-51 into Tokyo Bay. A B-17G of the 4th Emergency Rescue Squadron had dropped a wooden life-boat to Mikes, and the submarine *Aspro,* four Mustangs, two Privateers and a B-29 had all been involved in protecting the downed airman.

During the aerial engagement fought above Mikes, Morioka shot down 2Lt John J Coneff in a 457th FS P-51, although the pair of PB4Y-2s (from VPB-121) and the remaining Mustangs forced JNAF pilots to withdraw. However, before leaving the combat area, the four Zeroes twice strafed Capt Mikes in his life-boat, although he survived the harrowing ordeal with only few scratches from wood splinters.

On 13 August Morioka led eight Zeroes in an attack on a PBY which had landed in Tokyo Bay in an attempt to rescue a downed Hellcat pilot. Although the crew of the flying boat succeeded in taking off and racing at wave top height across the bay towards the open sea, they were eventually shot down near Tateyama, at the mouth of Tokyo Bay, following a brief chase.

On 15 August 1945 – just two hours before the surrender announce-

Lt(jg) Shiro Kurotori (right) and Tech/Lt(jg) Minoru Hida of the Yokosuka AG stand beside the impressive scoreboard painted onto the rear fuselage of their Gekko nightfighter – these victory markings were designed by Lt Cdr Yamada of the 7th Squadron. The aircraft's tail number (Yo-101) has been painted over (*via Robert C Mikesh*)

The same J1N1-S Gekko (Yo-101) seen in the previous photograph serves as backdrop for this shot of assorted Yokosuka AG air- and groundcrew (*via Robert C Mikesh*)

With its code just visible on the tail, this was the Gekko ('Irving') was flown by Lt(jg) Shiro Kurotori and CPO Juzo Kuramoto on the night of 25 May 1945 when the pair downed five B-29s and damaged a sixth. Note that the elaborate victory marks seen in the previous two photographs have not yet been applied (*K Osuo*)

ment – Lt Morioka achieved his fifth, and final, victory when he and seven comrades fought six F6F Hellcats of VF-88 in what was the last major dogfight between Hellcats and Zeroes in World War 2. He had bounced his victim at the start of the engagement, forcing the Hellcat pilot to take to his parachute. When Morioka and his crew chief went to visit the American three days later, they were turned away, for he had died of his wounds.

Becoming a certified practising accountant after the war, Yutaka Morioka credited his survival to veteran ace Akamatsu. On 4 December 1991, during the 50th Anniversary of the Pearl Harbor attack in Hawaii, he met Edward Mikes, whom he and his men had strafed 46 years earlier. The two old warriors shook hands and became the best of friends. Morioka died in July 1993.

# Lt(jg) Shiro Kurotori

Shiro Kurotori (whose surname means 'blackbird'), became an 'ace in-a-night', and an instant hero in Japan, in 1945.

Born in Tokyo in February 1923, young Shiro received his early flight training at Tsuchiura as a reconnaissance pilot, before switching to nightfighters when he was assigned to the Yokosuka AG. Here, he studied the techniques of Shigetoshi Kudo – one of the great nightfighting pioneers – and others who had returned from Rabaul.

Based on the experiences of the same veterans, the group prepared a Gekko with upward firing 20 mm cannon for Ens Kuratori and CPO Juzo Kuramoto. On the night of 15/16 April 1945, the pair sortied from Oppama airfield against B-29s from the 313th and 314th BW sent to attack Kawasaki and downed a Superfortress and damaged another.

The following month Kuratori and Kuramoto scored a spectacular success on the night of 25/26 May, their award citation, dated 1 June 1945, stating;

'Since December 1944, you participated in intercepting enemy planes attacking the mainland, downing six and damaging two others. You did a splendid job. Especially worthy was the results of 25 May 1945. At night, a big formation of B-29s came flying into the Kanto District. You piloted

A 332nd AG J1N1-Sa Type 2 Gekko Model 11 Ko is boarded in mid-March 1945 by its pilot, FPO1/c Nagano, and observer/aircraft commander Lt(jg) Tadashi Maniwa (*via Robert C Mikesh*)

A veritable 'sea' of JNAF single- and twin-engined types ground the Atsugi flightline in this late-1944 view. The five J1N1-Ss seen with their engines idling in the foreground belong to the 302nd AG (*via Robert C Mikesh*)

a Gekko and bravely attacked the waves of bombers, from south-west of Kanto to the north-east. In the fight lasting three hours, you downed five and damaged one. By your distinguished service, you contributed to the defence of the Imperial land. I hereby recognise your military merit and your deeds will be cited in the Naval All Units Proclamation.'

The citation was issued by the Adm Michitaro Tozuka, CO of the Yokosuka Naval Air Station. In addition to the citation, the team of Kuratori and Kuramoto also received ceremonial swords in recognition of their actions, and the former was promoted to lieutenant (junior grade) on 1 June. His CO also forbade him to intentionally ram a B-29.

Lt(jg) Kuratori was still training for the final decisive air battle when the war came to an abrupt end. He had achieved six B-29 victories.

A6M Model 52s of the 653rd AG (a mixed fighter and reconnaissance group) undergo maintenance at an overcrowded Oita airfield in August 1944 (*via Aerospace Publishing*)

Lt Chitoshi Isozaki was a great instructor who produced many aces – one of his most successful students was Ens Saburo Sakai. He is shown here at Meiji Airfield in December 1944 whilst serving with the 302nd AG. He finished the war flying Shiden-Kai fighters with the elite 343rd AG in home defence missions (*Sakaida*)

# APPENDICES

## Flying Units of the JNAF

The flying units of the JNAF were organised much like their opposite numbers within the Allied air forces. Japan's navy and army had their own air services, there being no independent air force like the German *Luftwaffe* or the British Royal Air Force.

The working component of the JNAF was the Air Group (*Kokutai*). *Kokutai* is used to denote JNAF air groups whereas *Sentai* is used for the JAAF. There were about 90 air groups within the JNAF, and depending on the size of the unit, these controlled between 36-64 (or more) aircraft.

Air Groups were either identified by names or numbers. Named groups are associated with a particular air command or base (Yokosuka Air Group, Sasebo Air Group). With a few exceptions such as the Tainan Air Group, most units that went overseas dropped their names and were given number designations (Kanoya Air Group became the 253rd Air Group for example). Air groups with numbers between 200 and 399 were fighter units, whilst those in the 600 to 699 range controlled a mix of aircraft. Floatplane units were numbered between 400 and 499. Carriers were too small to accommodate entire air groups, so the units on board took their names from the vessel they were embarked on (*Shokaku* Fighter Squadron for example).

The Air Group was divided into three or four squadrons (*hikotai*), with each squadron having between 12 to 16 aircraft. It could be commanded by a lieutenant (junior grade), a warrant officer, or even an experienced chief petty officer.

The majority of the pilots were enlisted men and not officers, unlike many of their Allied counterparts. Contrary to popular belief, while many non-aviation officers did not associate with their enlisted subordinates, officer pilots went to great lengths to form a bond. Said one Zero pilot;:

'These green lieutenants didn't know how to fight and would get shot down right away. So he was assigned a veteran enlisted man to protect him. If he was unpopular, the wingman might become "separated" during combat and the officer would surely die. *Do you understand*?'

The smallest operational unit in the squadron was the flight or section (*shotai*), which consisted of between three and four aircraft – four flights were usually found in the squadron. Initially, the flight consisted of three aircraft.

However, Lt Zenjiro Miyano was the first to effectively copy and refine the four-fighter flight formation from the Americans in 1943. Positions one and three were flown by seasoned veterans, while positions two and four were occupied by neophytes. This combination assured a higher rate of survival for the new pilot, plus allowed him to learn critical combat skills from his mentor. By 1944, the three-fighter flight had been mostly discarded. Through hard experience, it had been found that the 'odd man out' in a three-fighter flight usually became separated in combat and was shot down.

## JNAF Air Groups of World War 2

The following list of naval air groups is not presented in numeric order since the establishment of the units was not carried out sequentially. Only fighter air groups of any significance are listed – carrier squadrons are not listed.

### Yokosuka
Established 4/30 at Yokosuka. Japan's first naval Air Group fought over Iwo Jima and participated in the home defence. Disbanded at the end of the war

### Chitose - 201st
Established 10/39 at Chitose, Japan. Reorganised as the 201st AG 12/42 at Roi, Marshall Islands. Reorganised again 3/44, disbanded at the end of the war

### Kanoya - 253rd
Established 4/36 at Kanoya, Japan. The unit helped sink the British battleship HMS *Prince of Wales*. Reorganised 11/42 as 253rd AG. Fought at Rabaul and in the Solomons. Disbanded 7/44

### Genzan - 252nd
Established 11/40 at Genzan (Wonsan), Korea. Participated in the Battle of the Coral Sea. Renamed 252nd AG 9/42, disbanded at end of war

### 1st
Established 4/41 at Kanoya, Japan. Fought briefly in China. Disbanded 9/41

**Tainan - 251st**

Established 10/41 at Tainan, Formosa. The was the most famous JNAF unit due to its spectacular early successes, it also boasted the most aces, including Saburo Sakai and Hiroyoshi Nishizawa. Reorganised 11/42 as 251st AG. Disbanded 7/44

**3rd - 202nd**

Established 4/41. First unit to be composed solely of fighter aircraft. It gained a fierce reputation during the early months of the war. Participated in the attacks over the Philippines, Dutch East Indies and Darwin, Australia. Reorganised as 202nd AG 11/42, disbanded 7/44

**4th**

Established 2/42 on the island of Truk and saw duty over Rabaul and eastern New Guinea. The unit was merged with Tainan Kokutai 4/42

**2nd - 582nd**

Established 5/42 at Yokosuka Air Base, Japan. Active over eastern New Guinea and Guadalcanal. Reorganised as 582nd AG, it had claimed around 220 victories when the fighter unit was disbanded 7/43

**6th - 204th**

Established 4/42 at Kisarazu Air Base, Japan. Participated in the attacks at Dutch Harbor (Aleutians), Battle of Midway, eastern New Guinea and Rabaul. Reorganised as 204th AG 11/42. Disbanded 4/44. From inception till the end, the unit claimed over 1000 aerial victories

**281st**

Established 2/43 at Maizuru Air Base, Japan. Saw limited service in the northern Kurile Islands, then transferred to the Marshall Islands and Rabaul. Unit was totally destroyed by 2/44, their pilots fighting as infantrymen during the invasion of Kwajalein and Roi (Marshall Islands). The top JNAF ace, Tetsuzo Iwamoto, saw much action with this unit

**261st**

Established 6/43 at Kagoshima Air Base, Japan. Fought over Peleliu Island, Saipan and Yap. Disbanded 7/44

**331st**

Established 7/43 at Saeki Air Base in Japan. Limited actions in Burma and Calcutta, and also fought over Borneo and the Philippines. Disbanded 5/44

**254th**

Established 10/43, provided air defence for Hainan Island and Hong Kong. Later fought over Formosa and in the Philippines, where it was destroyed in heavy fighting. Disbanded 1/45

**263rd**

Established 10/43 at Genzan, Korea. Fought over Tinian, Peleliu and Guam. Disbanded 7/44

**321st**

Established 10/43 at Mobara Air Base, Japan. First JNAF nightfighter unit. Fought over Tinian and Guam. Disbanded 7/44

**381st**

Established 10/43. Fought over Biak, Borneo, Celebes and French Indochina. Disbanded at the end of the war

**265th**

Established 11/43 at Kagoshima Air Base, Japan. Fought at Saipan and the Marianas. Disbanded 7/44

**301st**

Established 11/43 at Yokosuka Naval Base, Japan. Fought at Tinian and Iwo Jima. Destroyed at Iwo Jima and disbanded 7/44

**341st**

Established 11/43 at Matsuyama Air Base, Japan. Fought over Iwo Jima, Formosa and the Philippines using the new Shiden ('George') fighter. Some pilots flew *kamikaze* suicide attacks. The unit had been destroyed in the Philippines by 1/45

**153rd**

Established 1/44, fought over western New Guinea. Reorganised as a reconnaissance and nightfighter unit 7/44. Disbanded at the end of the war

**343rd**

Established 1/44 at Matsuyama Air Base, Japan. Fought at Guam, disbanded 7/44. Second formation established 12/44 at Matsuyama as an elite unit of hand-picked veterans flying the Shiden-Kai. Disbanded at the end of the war

**221st**

Established 1/44 at Kasanbara Air Base, Japan. Fought over Formosa and the Philippines. By 1/45 unit was virtually annihilated

**256th**

Established 2/44 at Lunghwa airfield, Shanghai (China). Fought over Shanghai, Philippines and Formosa. Disbanded 12/44

**203rd**

Established 2/44 at Atsugi Air Base, Japan. Fought over the northern Kurile Islands of Japan, Okinawa, Philippines, Formosa and home defence. Disbanded at the end of the war

### 302nd

Established 3/44 at Kisarazu Air Base, Japan. Guarded the Imperial Capital against B-29 attacks and also fought over Okinawa. Disbanded at the end of the war

### 131st

Established 7/44 at Yokosuka Air Base, Japan. Fought over Okinawa and home defence. Disbanded at the end of the war

### 332nd

Established 8/44 at Iwakuni Air Base, Japan. Fought over the Philippines and home defence. Disbanded at the end of the war

### 352nd

Established 8/44 in Japan. Fought in the home defence, disbanded at the end of the war

### 210th

Established 9/44 at Meiji Air Base, Japan. Fought at Okinawa and the home defence, disbanded at the end of the war

### 721st

Established 10/44 as a *kamikaze* suicide unit at Konoike Air Base, Japan. Flew suicide attack missions at Okinawa using Zeroes and piloted rocket bombs (Ohka). Disbanded at the end of the war

### 205th

Established 2/45 at Taichung Air Base, Formosa. Participated in *kamikaze* attacks at Okinawa. Disbanded at the end of the war

## Aerial Victory Claims by JNAF Pilots

In the American and Commonwealth custom, the shooting down of five or more enemy aircraft entitled the pilot to call himself (herself in the USSR) an 'ace'. He joined an elite fraternity of fighter pilots whose accomplishments were widely publicised in the military and national press. As the victories mounted, his achievements were recognised with the awarding of medals and promotion through the ranks.

Although the Japanese adopted many of the concepts of flight from the West (Europe in particular), in its culture, the trait of individuality, which was so valued in the West, was shunned. Since early school days, Japanese children are taught to work and sacrifice for the benefit of the group. In a military context, this often manifested itself in basic training – both before and during World War 2 – when drill instructor lined up their trainees and struck them

for the shortcomings of a single individual in the group. In war, teamwork was critical, and there could be no prima donnas. When an individual accomplished a distinguished feat, the group received the honours.

During the China War, and in the early part of the Pacific campaign when Japan was on the offensive, various units did record individual credits in their mission reports. However, in June 1943 navy GHQ issued a directive prohibiting the continuation of this practice, this measure being taken in an effort to promote greater teamwork – most units adhered to the new policy.

As with fighter pilots the world over, Japanese aviators *did* keep personal scores, and for morale purposes they would paint victory markings on the aircraft. Since pilots flew aircraft on an availability basis, the number of 'kill' markings on the aircraft could be deceptive, for it was the fighter, rather than the pilot, who scored the victory.

There was no established rule for determining a victory. Many pilots would claim the destruction of an enemy aircraft which was seen to smoke in the air, believing that it would never reach home. The Japanese did have gun cameras, but they were only used for training purposes. The claim was usually taken on face value and added to the group's score.

As the war turned against the Japanese, and surviving pilots fought with tenacity, trying to hit as many enemy aircraft as possible before their end, many simply stopped counting. Although a few leading aces received rare personal citations and ceremonial swords for outstanding service, in general pilots had no incentive to inflate their claims in the hop of winning such honours because they were literally fighting for their lives.

Despite this, claims by JNAF pilots cannot be taken at face value. The inflated totals resulted from both confusion in combat and from a very liberal method of scorekeeping. During the early part of the war, many pilots received official recognition from the government for their victories (taken from individual citations and unit reports), but this does not imply that these victories were 'confirmed'.

Postwar, Japanese historians have recognised the problem of inflated totals, and tried to compensate by systematically reducing the scores by percentages. WO Takeo Tanimizu claimed 32 victories during the war, but historians have reduced his score to 18. Likewise, the top JNAF ace, Lt(jg) Tetsuzo Iwamoto, claimed 202 victories, although his tally has now been reduced to 'about 80' – It is a fact that no Japanese pilot ever reached 100 victories.

Since there is no basis for verifying claims, the postwar reduction of scores seem arbitrary. Likewise, accepting the claims on face value would also be grossly inaccurate.

The following list of JNAF aces was compiled from numerous sources. These scores are simply unverified claims either made by the pilots or attributed to them. The numerical scores represent a mixture of confirmed, unconfirmed, probable, damaged and imagined victories.

# JNAF Aces Listings

| Rank | Name | Score |
| --- | --- | --- |
| Lt(jg) | Iwamoto, Tetsuzo | 202 |
| CPO | Sugita, Shoichi | 120+ |
| WO | Nishizawa, Hiroyoshi | 86 |
| WO | Fukumoto, Shigeo | 72 |
| Ens | Sakai, Saburo | 60+ |
| CPO | Okumura, Takeo | 54 |
| Lt(jg) | Sasai, Junichi | 54 |
| WO | Okabe, Kenji | 50 |
| Lt | Kanno, Naoshi | 48 |
| WO | Ohara, Ryoji | 48 |
| Lt Cdr | Fujita, Iyozoh | 42 |
| WO | Komachi, Sadamu | 40 |
| Ens | Muto, Kaneyoshi | 35 |
| PO1/c | Ota, Toshio | 34 |
| WO | Sugino, Kazuo | 32 |
| WO | Tanimizu, Takeo | 32 |
| Ens | Ishihara, Susumu | 30+ |
| CPO | Ishii, Shizuo | 28 |
| Lt(jg) | Akamatsu, Sadaaki | 27 |
| WO | Ogiya, Nobuo | 24 |
| CPO | Hidaka, Yoshimi | 20 |
| Lt(jg) | Sugio, Shigeo | 20 |
| PO3/c | Uto, Kazushi | 19 |
| CPO | Nagano, Kiichi | 19 |
| WO | Okano, Hiroshi | 19 |
| PO1/c | Nakase, Masayuki | 18 |
| Lt(jg) | Matsuba, Akio | 18 |
| Ens | Saito, Saburo | 18+ |
| CPO | Oki, Yoshio | 18 |
| Ens | Honda, Minoru | 17+ |
| Ens | Tanaka, Kuniyoshi | 17 |
| CPO | Masuyama, Masao | 17 |
| Lt(jg) | Kamihara, Keishu | 17 |
| WO | Ito, Kiyoshi | 17 |
| WO | Katsuki, Kiyomi | 16+ |
| CPO | Matsunaga, Eitoku | 16 |
| CPO | Matsunaga, Hidenori | 16 |
| WO | Takesuka, Toraichi | 16 |
| Lt | Miyano, Zenjiro | 16 |
| CPO | Nakajima, Bunkichi | 16 |
| WO | Nakaya, Yoshiichi | 16 |
| CPO | Kato, Kunimichi | 16 |
| Ens | Shiga, Masami | 16 |
| WO | Watanabe, Hideo | 16 |
| Ens | Nakakariya, Kunimori | 16 |
| Ens | Minami, Yoshimi | 15 |
| WO | Yoshino, Satoshi | 15 |
| WO | Nakamichi, Wataru | 15 |
| WO | Shibukawa, Shigeru | 15 |
| Lt Cdr | Suho, Motonari | 15 |
| WO | Tanaka, Minpo | 15 |
| CPO | Koyae, Kotaro | 15 |
| PO1/c | Endo, Masuaki | 14 |
| PO1/c | Yamazaki, Ichirobei | 14 |
| PO2/c | Yoshida, Mototsuna | 14 |
| Ens | Taniguchi, Masao | 14 |
| WO | Ozeki, Yukiharu | 14 |
| WO | Takahashi, Kenichi | 14 |
| WO | Koga, Kiyoto | 13 |
| Lt(jg) | Handa, Watari | 13 |
| Ens | Yamamoto, Akira | 13 |
| WO | Yamashita, Sahei | 13 |
| WO | Matsumura, Momoto | 13 |
| WO | Kuroiwa, Toshio | 13 |
| WO | Maeda, Hideo | 13 |
| CPO | Uehara, Sadao | 13 |
| WO | Miyazaki, Gitaro | 13 |
| Sup Sea | Shibagaki, Hiroshi | 13 |
| Ens | Kondo, Masaichi | 13 |
| PO1/c | Omori, Shigetaka | 13 |
| Lt(jg) | Hagiri, Matsuo | 13 |
| Ens | Miyazaki, Isamu | 13 |
| Lt(jg) | Koizumi, Fujikazu | 13 |
| WO | Shibayama, Sekizen | 13 |
| WO | Kashimura, Kanichi | 12 |
| PO1/c | Yoshimura, Keisaku | 12 |
| WO | Kanamaru, Takeo | 12 |
| CPO | Kikuchi, Tetsuo | 12 |
| PO1/c | Shimizu, Kiyoshi | 12 |
| Lt | Isozaki, Chitoshi | 12 |
| Lt | Yamaguchi, Sadao | 12 |
| Ens | Sasakibara, Masao | 12 |
| PO1/c | Odaka, Noritsura | 12 |
| Ens | Yamashita, Koshiro | 11 |
| CPO | Sekiya, Kiyoshi | 11 |
| WO | Yasui, Kozaburo | 11 |
| CPO | Yamamoto, Tomezo | 11 |
| Lt(jg) | Wajima, Yoshio | 11 |
| PO2/c | Ichioka, Matao | 11 |
| PO3/c | Kokubun, Takeichi | 11 |
| Lt(jg) | Hidaka, Hatsuo | 11 |
| WO | Oishi, Yoshio | 11 |
| Lt(jg) | Iwai, Tsutomu | 11 |
| CPO | Shirahama, Yoshijiro | 11 |
| WO | Hori, Mitsuo | 11 |
| Lt | Fukuda, Sumio | 11 |
| Ens | Kodaira, Yoshinao | 11 |
| WO | Yamamoto, Ichiro | 11 |
| WO | Kitahata, Saburo | 10+ |

| | | |
|---|---|---|
| WO | Sugiyama, Teruo | 10 |
| CPO | Tanaka, Jiro | 10 |
| CPO | Tanaka, Shinsaku | 10 |
| PO2/c | Banno, Takao | 10 |
| CPO | Ishii, Isamu | 10 |
| Ldg Sea | Hattori, Kazuo | 10+ |
| CPO | Nagahama, Yoshikazu | 10+ |
| PO2/c | Kurosawa, Seiichi | 10 |
| CPO | Hashiguchi, Yoshiro | 10+ |
| Lt | Shigematsu, Yasuhiro | 10+ |
| Lt | Kobayashi, Hohei | 10+ |
| Ens | Kagemitsu, Matsuo | 10+ |
| Ens | Takahashi, Shigeru | 10 |
| CPO | Sasai, Tomokazu | 10 |
| WO | Atake, Tomita | 10 |
| WO | Yoshida, Katsuyoshi | 10 |
| Cdr | Aioi, Takahide | 10 |
| CPO | Abe, Kenichi | 10 |
| PO1/c | Sakano, Takao | 10 |
| Lt(jg) | Mochizuki, Isamu | 9 |
| LCdr | Shirane, Ayao | 9 |
| WO | Sueda, Toshiyuki | 9 |
| PO1/c | Suzuki, Kiyonobu | 9 |
| PO1/c | Okamoto, Juzo | 9 |
| WO | Oda, Kiichi | 9 |
| Lt(jg) | Mori, Mitsugu | 9 |
| Lt(jg) | Tsunoda, Kazuo | 9 |
| Lt(jg) | Morinio, Hideo | 9 |
| Lt(jg) | Matsuda, Jiro | 9 |
| Lt(jg) | Harada, Kaname | 9 |
| PO2/c | Izumi, Hideo | 9 |
| PO3/c | Matsuki, Susumu | 9 |
| WO | Nakamura, Yoshio | 9 |
| PO2/c | Kanda, Saji | 9 |
| Ens | Yamanaka, Tadao | 9 |
| PO1/c | Shirakawa, Toshihisa | 9 |
| CPO | Yoshizawa, Tokushige | 9 |
| CPO | Ishida, Teigo | 9 |
| Lt(jg) | Higashiyama, Ichiro | 9 |
| Lt | Fukui, Yoshio | 9 |
| WO | Kato, Katsue | 9 |
| Ens | Kudo, Shigetoshi | 9 |
| Lt Cdr | Kaneko, Tadashi | 8 |
| Lt | Iizuka, Masao | 8 |
| Lt(jg) | Ono, Takeyoshi | 8 |
| Lt | Nakagawa, Kenji | 8 |
| Lt | Endo, Yukio | 8+ |
| PO3/c | Moriura, Toyoo | 8 |
| CPO | Suzuki, Hiroshi | 8 |
| PO1/c | Takaiwa, Kaoru | 8 |
| PO1/c | Iwaki, Yoshio | 8 |

| | | |
|---|---|---|
| WO | Ema, Yuichi | 8 |
| PO1/c | Magara, Koichi | 8 |
| WO | Shigemi, Katsuma | 8 |
| PO1/c | Goto, Kurakazu | 8 |
| PO1/c | Yano, Shigeru | 8 |
| WO | Tokuji, Yoshihisa | 8 |
| Lt(jg) | Ono, Satoru | 8 |
| Ens | Muranaka, Kazuo | 8 |
| Lt | Nango, Mochifumi | 8 |
| CPO | Yoshihara, Hiroji | 8 |
| WO | Yanagiya, Kenji | 8 |
| Ens | Nakano, Katsujiro | 7 |
| Lt Cdr | Shiga, Yoshio | 6 |
| A1/c | Yonekawa, Tadayoshi | 6 |
| Lt(jg) | Kuratori, Shiro | 6 |
| WO | Hayashi, Sakuji | 6 |
| Lt | Oshibuchi, Takashi | 6 |
| CPO | Sasaki, Yoshiichi | 6 |
| Lt | Nishiwaki, Masaharu | 5+ |
| Lt | Hayashi, Yoshishige | 5 |
| PO | Mitsuda, Masahiro | 5 |
| Lt | Yokoyama, Tamotsu | 5 |
| CPO | Naka, Yoshimitsu | 5 |
| Lt | Morioka, Yutaka | 5 |
| PO1/c | Tsujinoue, Toyomitsu | 5 |
| PO1/c | Arita, Yoshisuke | 5 |
| WO | Takenaka, Yoshihiko | 5 |
| CPO | Ishikawa, Seiji | 5 |
| PO2/c | Kakimoto, Enji | 5 |

## COLOUR PLATES

**1**
**A5M2a Type 96 Model 2-1 of the 13th AG, flown by PO1/c Tetsuzo Iwamoto, Nanjing, China, February 1938**
The white unit marking '4' was used by the 13th AG between October 1937 and November 1940. Iwamoto noted in his diary that '4-133' was a distinguished aircraft which he flew from the first days of the China War, and in every major engagement he fought in. He also wrote that it had the most victories in the unit. This Type 96 was flown by many pilots.

**2**
**A5M2a Type 96 Model 2-1 of the 15th AG, flown by Lt Mochifumi Nango, Anjing, China, July 1938**
The white unit marking '10' was used by the 15th AG from June through to November 1938, whilst the white fuselage band indicates a flight leader. On 18 July 1938 Lt Nango was killed in this fighter when he collided with an I-15 over Lake Poyang during a bomber escort mission to Nanchang.

**3**
**A5M4 Type 96 Model 4 of the *Soryu* Fighter Sqn, flown by PO2/c Hideo Oishi, East China Sea, November 1938**

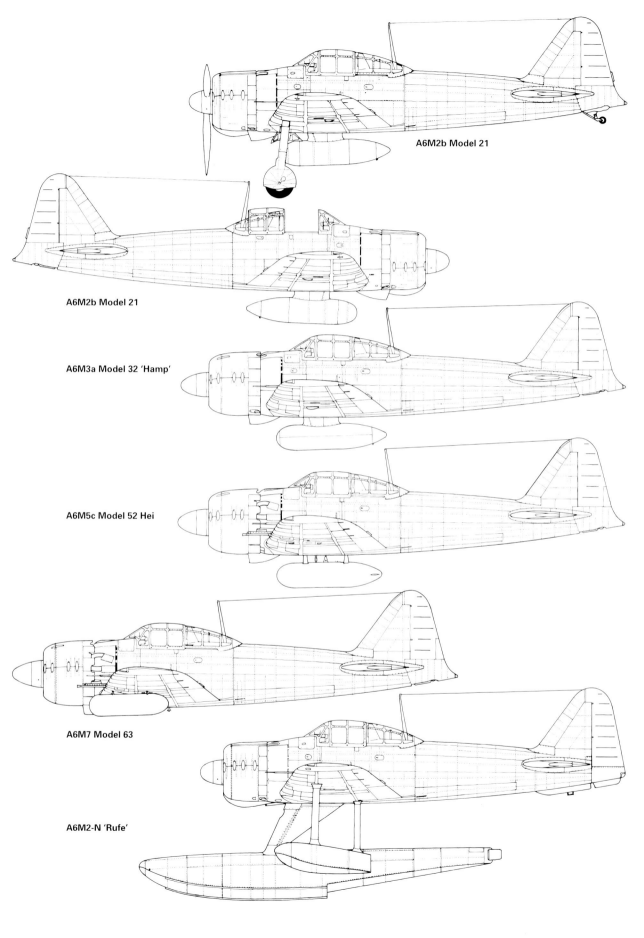

A6M2b Model 21

A6M2b Model 21

A6M3a Model 32 'Hamp'

A6M5c Model 52 Hei

A6M7 Model 63

A6M2-N 'Rufe'

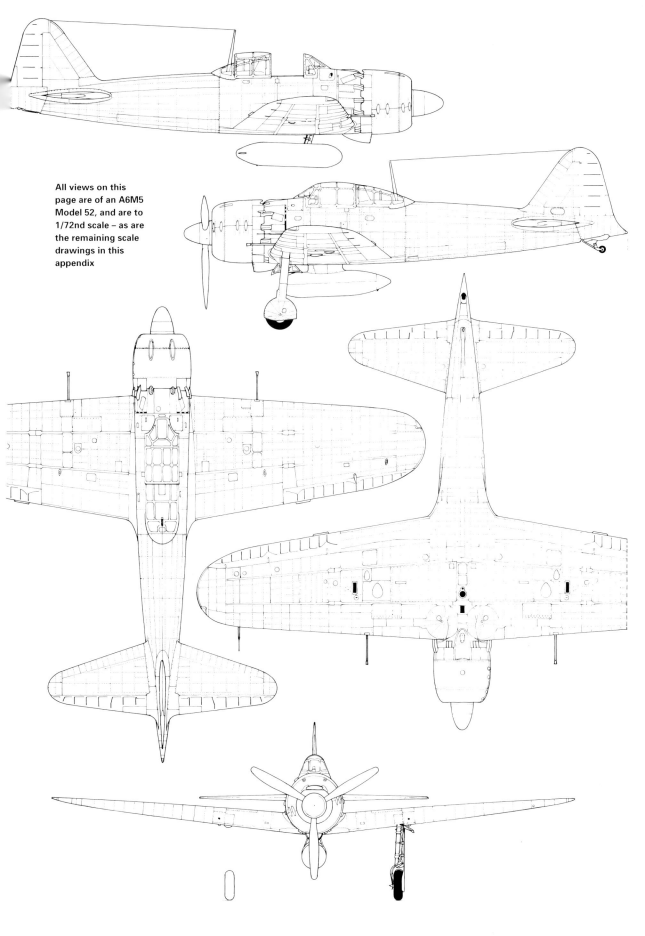

All views on this
page are of an A6M5
Model 52, and are to
1/72nd scale – as are
the remaining scale
drawings in this
appendix

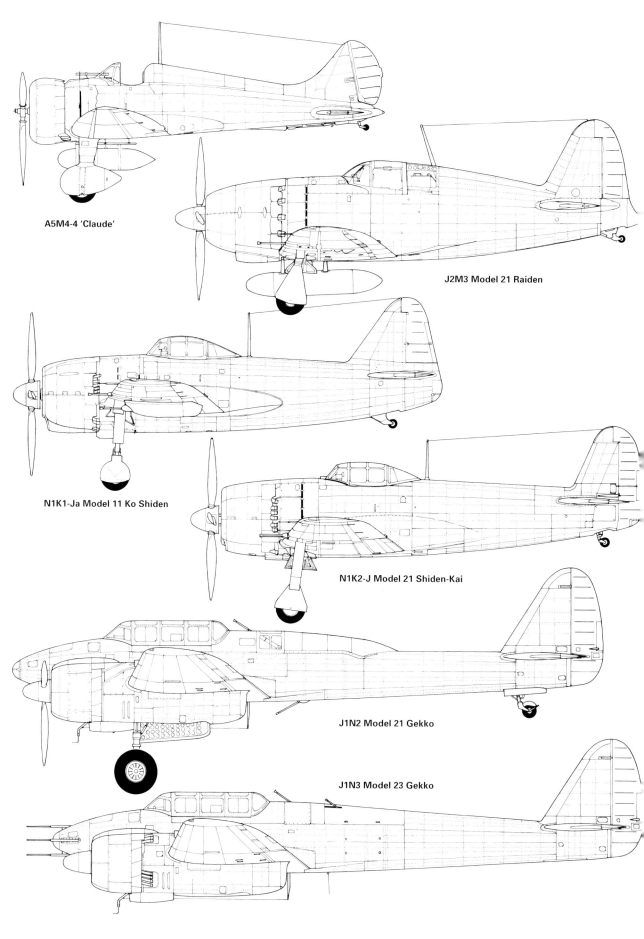

A5M4-4 'Claude'

J2M3 Model 21 Raiden

N1K1-Ja Model 11 Ko Shiden

N1K2-J Model 21 Shiden-Kai

J1N2 Model 21 Gekko

J1N3 Model 23 Gekko

The unit designation 'W' was used from the end of 1937 through to 1940. The inscription on the fuselage indicates that this fighter was presentation aircraft No 266, purchased by a Mr Iwai and donated to the navy – a common practice during the China War and the first months of the Pacific war.

## 4
### A5M4 Type 96 Model 4 of *Soryu* Fighter Squadron, flown by PO1/c Matsuo Hagiri, Japan, summer 1939

With a maximum speed of 270 mph at 9845 ft, the Type 96 could fly circles around the new Zero fighter – in mock dog-fights, the '96 won every time. Matsuo Hagiri went on to enjoy a distinguished career during World War 2.

## 5
### A6M2 Model 11 of the 12th AG, flown by WO Koshiro Yamashita, Hankow, China, 1940

The 12the AG used the number '3' as their unit designation, followed by the individual aircraft number, in 1940-41. The distinctive red swallow in a circle victory markings were frequently found on many of their Zeroes during this period.

## 6
### A6M2 Model 11 of the 12th AG, flown by squadron leader Lt Minoru Suzuki, Hankow, China, 1940

This fighter was flown by numerous pilots (including Lt Suzuki), most of whom contributed to the 28 victories painted on its tail. This high-scoring Zero was returned to Japan and exhibited at the Naval Academy after its tour of China ended in in late 1940. Lt Cdr Suzuki finished the war as a squadron leader in the 205th AG in Formosa, having scored eight kills.

## 7
### A6M2 Model 11 of the 12th AG, flown by PO2/c Tsutomu Iwai, Hankow, China, 13 September 1940

During the famous engagement over Hankow on this date, 13 Zeroes destroyed 27 enemy fighters without suffering a single loss – Iwai downed two. He later served in almost every theatre of the Pacific War, including home defence, and lived to see the end of the conflict, having scored 11+ victories.

## 8
### A6M2 Model 11 of the 12th AG, flown by PO2/c Hideo Oishi, Hankow, China, 1941

Although the radio equipment in the Zero was virtually useless from the word go due to static, there was no need for pilots to remove them (as in later years) in order to reduce weight. Oishi had achieved six victories before he was killed in aerial combat over the Philippines on 12 September 1944.

## 9
### A6M2 Model 11 of the 12th AG, flown by PO1/c Masayuki Nakase, Hankow, China, 14 March 1941

On this date young novice Nakase downed six Soviet I-152s in his first action, becoming one of the early JNAF 'ace-in-a-day' pilots. His total ammunition expenditure amounted to just 110 rounds of 20 mm cannon shell and 575 7.7 mm machine-gun bullets – Nakase later gained another three victories in China. On 9 February 1942 he became one of the first JNAF aces killed during World War 2 when his aircraft was shot down by ground fire during a strafing attack on

armoured cars in the Celebes. The 18-victory ace received a double posthumous promotion to the rank of ensign.

## 10
### A6M2 Model 21 of the Tainan AG, flown by Airman 1/c Masaaki Shimakawa, Formosa, October 1941

The Tainan AG utilised both the 'V' unit designation (from October 1941 through to October 1942) and a diagonal fuselage stripe to marking their Zeroes. This aircraft was further personalised through the addition of the kanji character 'Shima' inside the red sun emblem on the fuselage – this was a temporary marking made from crushed chalk and water, and it served as aid to identifying the pilot during carrier landings (training) and long-range flights. Each pilot in the squadron painted the first kanji of his surname onto his aircraft.

## 11
### A6M2 Model 21 of the 3rd AG, flown by PO2/c Yoshiro Hashiguchi, Dutch East Indies, February 1942

The 'X' unit designation was used by the 3rd AG from April 1941 through to October 1942. Various pilots flew 'X-183', adding their victories to its score, although most of the kills were achieved by Hashiguchi. He later fought in the Solomons and the Philippines, where he met his death on 25 October 1944 having scored over ten victories.

## 12
### A6M2 Model 21 of the Tainan AG, flown by PO2/c Susumu Ishihara, Surabaya, Java, February 1942

Ishihara flew this aircraft during the Dutch East Indies campaign, performing mostly ground attack and patrol roles. He later saw considerable action in the Solomons battles and ended the war with over 30 victories.

## 13
### A6M2 Model 21 of the Tainan AG, flown by PO2/c Yoshisuke Arita, Bali, February 1942

This presentation aircraft was flown by Arita prior to his death in aerial combat over Port Moresby on 1 May 1942.

## 14
### A6M2 Model 21 of the Tainan AG, flown by PO1/c Saburo Sakai, Rabaul, 7 August 1942

Wearing the white tail stripe of a flight leader, 'V-128' was the mount of CPO Sakai during his eventful long-range mission to Guadalcanal on 7 August. He claimed three kills during the sortie, but was also seriously wounded by SBD gunners from VB-6. Given up for dead, Sakai flew for nearly five hours before gliding his Zero into Rabaul's Lakunai airfield out of fuel.

## 15
### F1M2 Type Zero Observation Seaplane Model 11 of the seaplane tender *Chitose*, flown by PO1/c Kiyomi Katsuki (pilot) and PO2/c Michio Takarada, 4 October 1942

Although the biplane *fighter* era ended with the introduction of the Type 96, the F1M2 (codenamed 'Pete') was nevertheless produced in quantity during World War 2. The team of Katsuki and Takarada were flying 'Y1-23' on 4 October 1942 when they rammed and destroyed a B-17 which was about to attack the seaplane carrier *Nisshin*.

## 16

**A6M2 Model 21 of the *Shokaku* Fighter Squadron, flown by squadron leader Lt Hideki Shingo during the Battle of Santa Cruz, 26 October 1942**

Lt Shingo led his Zeroes in the second wave attack on the US Task Force, during which they claimed five aircraft shot down. The tail code designation 'EI' was used from September 1941 through to October 1942. Shingo survived the war and later became a jet fighter pilot in the Japan Self Defense Air Force.

## 17

**A6M2 Model 21 of the Oppama AG, flown by CPO Tetsuzo Iwamoto, Kanagawa Prefecture, Japan, 1/43**

Following the loss of many veteran pilots at Midway, Iwamoto was pulled out of combat in August 1942 and sent home to become an instructor. In November of that same year a JNAF directive redesignated all named land-based units going overseas with numbers. The unit designation on this aircraft (written in Japanese phonetic characters and preceding its number '101') reads O-Hee (Oppama Aviation).

## 18

**A6M2 Model 21 of the *Zuikaku* Fighter Squadron, flown by CPO Saburo Saito, Rabaul, January 1943**

Th *Zuikaku* Fighter Squadron was reorganised following the carrier's return to Japan after the Battle of Santa Cruz (October 1942). The unit designation 'A1-1' replaced 'E11', and was used until November 1943. The squadron assisted in the evacuation of Guadalcanal, before being temporarily based ashore at Rabaul and Buin. Saito scored his first victory on 1 February 1943 when he jointly shot down a Wildcat of VMF-112 near Savo Island. He was wounded on 24 October 1944 near Luzon and never flew again, having scored over 18 victories and completed 2118 flying hours.

## 19

**A6M2-N Type 2 Floatplane Fighter of the 802nd AG, flown by Lt(jg) Keizo Yamazaki, Shortland Island Seaplane Base, February 1943**

Codenamed 'Rufe' by the Allies, this aircraft was one of two successful floatplane designs utilised by the JNAF, the great benefit of this type of fighter being its ability to be based almost anywhere along an island coastline – tents would provide housing for pilots and groundcrew. On 13 February 1943 Lt(jg) Yamazaki claimed a P-39 probable flying this fighter, whilst various other pilots also enjoyed success with it – these kills were marked with small red hatchets on the tail.

## 20

**A6M3 Model 22 of the 251st AG, flown by CPO Hiroyoshi Nishizawa, Aichi Prefecture, Japan, Spring 1943**

The unit designation 'UI' was used from 1942 through to June 1943, during which time Nishizawa flew this aircraft as an instructor.

## 21

**A6M3 Model 32 of the 204th AG, flown by PO2/c Kenji Yanagiya, Buin, 18 April 1943**

Yanagiya flew 'T2-169' on the ill-fated Adm Yamamoto escort mission, during which he claimed a P-38 probable. Note that this aircraft lacks a radio mast, which has been cut off in order

to save weight. Unshielded ignitions in the engine interfered with radio reception, rendering it virtually worthless – pilots also discarded the radio equipment too. Understanding commanders did nothing to stop the practice.

## 22

**A6M3 Model 22 of the 204th AG, flown by WO Matsuo Hagiri, Buin, summer 1943**

Hagiri had shot down six enemy aircraft during his two-month stay with this unit., before being wounded in aerial combat with F4U Corsairs and RNZAF P-40s on 23 September 1943 over Kahili. Prior to being hit he had claimed two victories. Hagiri subsequently returned to Japan for hospitalisation.

## 23

**A6M3 Model 22 of the 204th AG, flown by PO2/c Shoichi Sugita, Rabaul, June 1943**

Even experienced pilots like Sugita did not have their own assigned aircraft, flying whatever fighter was available at the time. During the month of June he destroyed or damaged two F4Fs, three F4Us and three unspecified aircraft.

## 24

**A6M3 Model 22 of the 201st AG, flown by CPO Takeo Okumura, Buin, September 1943**

The unit designation 'WI' was used from June 1943 through to 1944, during which time CPO Okumura set the JNAF record for shooting down the most number of enemy aircraft in a single day – ten on 14 September 1943 over Buin.

## 25

**A6M2-N Type 2 Floatplane Fighter, 934th AG, flown by CPO Eitoku Matsunaga, Banda Sea/Ambon Island, September 1943-44**

Reputedly the top floatplane ace of the Pacific War with eight kills, Matsunaga survived the war and has since shunned publicity, thus relegating his career into historical obscurity.

## 26

**N1K1-J Shiden 11 of the 341st AG, 402nd Squadron, the Philippines, mid-1944**

The 341st AG was to be armed with the new Shiden fighter in 1943, but due to production delays it did not receive its first aircraft until February 1944. A modified and further developed land-based version of the 'Rex' floatplane, the Shiden was modified extensively, and finally gained acceptance into JNAF service. Despite the 'George's' highly-regarded automatic combat flap system, it was plagued by engine and undercarriage problems, leading Lt Iyozoh Fujita, Midway air hero and division officer of the 402nd Squadron, to sum the much-touted fighter up with just two words – 'No good!'

## 27

**A6M3 Model 32 of the Tainan AG, flown by CPO Takeo Tanimizu, Tainan, Formosa, September 1944**

This aircraft belonged to an operational training unit, rather than the famous Tainan AG, which was active over New Guinea in 1942. The unit designation in phonetic characters read Tai, followed by the aircraft number '184'. Tanimizu was flying this aircraft on the night of 31 August 1944 when he downed B-24 44-40783 of the 425th BS/308th BG, flown by

1Lt Norman B Clendenen. The kanji inscriptions on the rear fuselage reads, 'Combat diary. 31 August 1944, participated in combat over Takao. 3 September, the same. Downed one B-24'. Pilots rarely had inscriptions painted on their aircraft, Tanimizu doing so to encourage his inexperienced comrades.

## 28

**J2M3 Raiden 21 of the 302nd AG, flown by Lt(jg) Sadaaki Akamatsu, Atsugi airfield, March 1944 to August 1945**

Akamatsu flew this aircraft both on training flights and in combat, the victory markings on its tail indicating that the Raiden had received the credit for these successes, not the pilot.

## 29

**N1K2-J Shiden-Kai 21 of the 343rd AG, 701st Squadron, flown by squadron leader Lt Takashi Oshibuchi, Kyushu, April 1945**

The letter 'C' on the tail of this 'George' denotes that it belongs to the 701st Squadron, whilst the double red diagonal fuselage stripes indicate a squadron leader's aircraft. On 16 April 1945 Oshibuchi led 32 'Georges' to Okinawa during the No 3 Kikusui Operation, the fighters subsequently claiming 20 F6Fs destroyed for the loss of nine N1K2-Js. Oshibuchi was killed on 24 July 1945 in '343-C-13' when he was downed by VF-49's Lt George M Williams over the Bungo Straits.

## 30

**J1N1-S Model 21 of the 302nd AG, 2nd Squadron, flown by Lt Yukio Endo (pilot) and CPO Osamu Nishio (observer), Atsugi airfield, January 1945**

This Gekko's victory markings consist of five double cherry blossoms (destroyed) and nine single blossoms (probables), these successes having been achieved by Endo and Nishio. At the time of their deaths on 14 January 1945, the pair had been credited with at least eight B-29 victories.

## 31

**A6M5 Model 52 of the 252nd AG, 311th Squadron, flown by Ens Tetsuzo Iwamoto, Mobara airfield, Japan, 16 February 1945**

On this day US carrier aircraft raided the Tokyo region, Iwamoto leading eight Zeroes of his squadron in counterattack against F4U Corsairs. Before the day ended, he had claimed seven destroyed and one damaged.

## 32

**A6M5 Model 52 of the 302nd AG, flown by Ens Sadaaki Akamatsu, Atsugi airfield, Japan, 16-17 February 1945**

Capable of speeds of up to 351 mph at 19,685 ft, the Model 52 was rushed into combat during the autumn of 1943, and in the hands of veteran pilots proved to be a match for the F6F and F4U. During the two-day carrier attacks on Tokyo Akamatsu used this Zero to claim four Hellcats kills – as indicated by the chrysanthemum victory markings. The two cherry blossom markings indicate damaged claims.

## 33

**J2M3 Raiden 21 of the 352nd AG, flown by Lt(jg) Yoshihiro Aoki, Omura airfield, March 1945**

Formed in August 1944 to protect the Sasebo, Nagasaki and Omura areas, this unit was called Kusanagi (Heavenly Scythe),

but it did not live up to its name. Reserve Lt(jg) Aoki served as a division officer within the 352nd AG, heading the Raiden unit in attacks on B-29s. Extraneous markings such as these lightning bolts were rare on JNAF aircraft.

## 34

**N1K2-J Shiden-Kai of the 343rd AG, 407th Squadron, of CPO Hideo Nakao, Matsuyama airfield, Japan, 3/45**

The number '20' in the red 'meatball' indicates that this aircraft was used for training prior to combat. The Shiden-Kai carried two 20 mm Type 99 Mark 4 cannon in each wing, with a rate of fire of over 490 rpm. Each cannon was belt-fed from a magazine which held 250 rounds, although pilots felt that the weapons' fired too slowly.

## 35

**J2M3 Raiden 21 of the 302nd AG, 1st Squadron, flown by Lt Susumu Ito, Atsugi airfield, April 1945**

The fuselage band indicates that this aircraft was flown by a flight leader, and the kill markings on the upper tail comprise four chrysanthemums (definite) and one cherry blossom (probable or damaged). The kanji characters beneath the 'Yo-D (for Yokosuka Defence) 152' read 'Maintenance PO1/c Fukuda', who was its mechanic. Ito was the 2nd Division leader.

## 36

**N1K2-J Shiden-Kai 21 of the 343rd AG, 301st Squadron, flown by CPO Katsue Kato, Matsuyama airfield, 4/45**

The white '02' marking was a temporary number used for training purposes, this aircraft being flown by CPO Katsue Kato on 16 April 1945 from Matsuyama. This aircraft was one of 32 'Georges' sortied during the No 3 Kikusui Operation (special attack) to Okinawa, Kato being killed in this action.

## 37

**J2M3 Raiden 21 of the 332nd AG's Tatsumaki Unit, flown by WO Susumu Ishihara, Kanoya Air Base, 27 April 1945**

The '32' on the tail denotes the last two digits of the 332nd AG, this group being organised for the defence of Kure. Ishihara achieved 16 officially recognised kills before individual credits were abolished – his score stood at 30+ by war's end.

## 38

**N1K2-J Shiden-Kai 21 of the Yokosuka AG, flown by Ens Kaneyoshi Muto, April 1945**

The backward 'E' on the tail is a Japanese phonetic katakana (writing), pronounced 'Yo' (for Yokosuka Defence). The unit had several such aircraft for test and evaluation purposes.

## 39

**N1K2-J Shiden-Kai 21 of the 343rd AG, 407th Squadron, flown by WO Isamu Miyazaki, Kyushu, April 1945**

The letter 'B' denotes the 407th Squadron, whilst the white diagonal stripe shows that this aircraft was flown by a flight leader.The Shiden-Kai boasted armour protection, and US pilots noted in their mission reports that it was very difficult to set one on fire, unlike the Zero.

## 40

**N1K2-J Shiden-Kai 21 of the 343rd AG, 301st Squadron,**

flown by squadron leader Lt Naoshi Kanno, Matsuyama airfield, Japan, April 1945

The letter 'A' denotes the 301st Squadron, whilst the number '15', painted inside the red 'meatball', was temporary for training and maintenance purposes – it was never used during combat missions. Lt Kanno flew 'A15' during the No 3 Kikusui Operation to Okinawa on 16 April 1945.

## 41

**J1N1-S Gekko Model 23 of the Yokosuka AG, 7th Squadron, flown by CPO Juzo Kuramoto (pilot) and Ens Shiro Kurotori (observer), Yokosuka airfield, May 1945**

Adorned on the rear fuselage are eight victory markings (six probables and two destroyed), Kuromoto and his observer claiming five B-29s destroyed and one damaged in this aircraft on the night of 25 May 1945.

## 42

**A6M5 Model 52 of the 203rd AG, 303rd Squadron, flown by CPO Takeo Tanimizu, Kagoshima Prefecture, Japan, June 1945**

The unusual kill markings on this aircraft made it the most celebrated Zero ever depicted in postwar publications. The two head-on silhouettes of B-29s represent one probable and another jointly shot down with CPO Tetsuzo Iwamoto. The five stars with arrows indicate kills, whilst the single unpierced star denotes a probable or damaged aircraft. Tanimizu had these markings painted on to inspire his inexperienced men. The broken up hulk of this aircraft was photographed in a Nagasaki hangar in November 1945.

## 43

**A6M7 Model 63 of the 302nd AG, flown by squadron leader Lt Yutaka Morioka, Atsugi airfield, Japan, 3/8/45**

Lt Morioka flew No 106 (accompanied by three wingmen) in a desperate attempt to thwart the rescue of P-51 pilot Capt Ed Mikes Jr of the 458th FS, who had parachuted into Tokyo Bay. Morioka downed 2Lt John J Coneff of the 457th FS, who had been covering Mikes, and before returning to base from their unsuccessful sortie, he and his men strafed the American pilot in his life-boat, although Mikes escaped with minor splinter wounds.

# FIGURE PLATES

## 1

This is what the completely outfitted carrier pilot looked like in 1941-42. PO3/c Sadamu Komachi is seen ready for action whilst serving aboard *Shokaku* at the time of the Pearl Harbor raid, wearing his one-piece winter flightsuit, which was waterproofed, but not fireproof, and trimmed with a white rabbit fur collar. His headgear comprised a woollen toque and winter helmet, whilst over his kapok life jacket (which offered its wearer some protection from flying shrapnel) he wears a Type 97 parachute harness with a white cloth name tag on the right vertical strap. Komachi's gauntlets, which are stuffed into his right leg pocket, are made from deerskin.

## 2

After having had his hand amputated by the tail gunner of a B-29 in January 1945, Lt Yutaka Morioka of the 302nd AG returned to duty sporting an iron claw! He is seen wearing an early style (button sleeve) brown gabardine summer flightsuit and a winter (rabbit fur-lined) helmet. A small green cloth name patch is sewn onto his left breast, but it has been left unmarked (as was usually the case), for the suits were often reissued to other pilots. Home defence pilots like Morioka did not carry pistols unless their mission took them away from the Japanese mainland – to Iwo Jima or Okinawa, for example. A headphone cord dangles around his neck. JNAF aviators often wore silk scarves (often white, as they were usually made from salvaged parachutes, although other colours were occasionally seen) as part of their attire.

## 3

PO1/c Takeo Tanimizu wears typical JNAF flying gear whilst aboard the carrier *Junyo* in May 1942. He is attired in a one-piece brown gabardine summer flying suit, which is quilted inside (lined) for additional warmth while at sea. Tanimizu's kapok-filled life jacket is of an early style, boasting a small utility pocket which contains his watch. Many pilots carried a pistol, although this was not for personal protection, but instead to be used as an instrument with which to commit suicide in order to prevent capture – Tanimizu's is an 8 mm Nambu (Nagoya 1st series, produced in November 1941 and serialled 2147), which belonged to the carrier's arsenal. It had an eight-shot capacity, but only five rounds were loaded to prevent magazine spring weakness. Holsters were too bulky, so the usual method of securement was with a rope lanyard. In his hand is a summer issue gauntlet. Unusually for the 1942 period, Tanimizu is wearing a *hachimaki* (headband) – these were used both to keep the sweat from the pilot's eyes and to symbolise his manly spirit.

## 4

Winter and high altitude flying over Atsugi made heavy flying gear a must for flight instructor Lt(jg) Sadaaki Akamatsu of the 302nd AG in early 1945. The late style winter flightsuit (zippered sleeve as opposed to the early button sleeve) has a rabbit fur collar and is quilted inside. Of interest is the custom-made winter flying helmet worn by the pilot – some officer pilots, for whatever reason, had custom helmets specially made for them. The standard issue item was made from sheepskin. Akamatsu wears typical short black flying boots with leather soles and rubber heels.

## 5

Just back from the China War, newly-promoted PO1/c Kaneyoshi Muto of the 12th AG gives off the impression of being a seasoned veteran in his petty officer's blues. On his left breast are three medals – the Golden Kite, Rising Sun 1st Class and the China Incident medal. On the lower right-hand side of Muto's tunic is an air medal, whilst his right sleeve carries two *Zenkosho* (good conduct stripes) and a sleeve rating depicting a naval aviator, Petty Officer 1st Class.

## 6

PO2/c Saburo Sakai of the 12th AG is depicted at Nanchang air base, in southern China in 1939. He is wearing typical two-piece tropical work fatigues and a floppy (but quite functional) 'Daisy Mae' hat. In the heat of the tropics pilots would wear these work clothes beneath their unlined summer flightsuits.